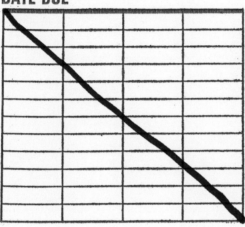

Planning
Colleges
for the
Community

Dorothy Knoell
Charles McIntyre

PLANNING
COLLEGES
FOR THE
COMMUNITY

Jossey-Bass Publishers
San Francisco · Washington · London · 1974

PLANNING COLLEGES FOR THE COMMUNITY
by Dorothy Knoell and Charles McIntyre

Copyright © 1974 by: Jossey-Bass, Inc., Publishers
615 Montgomery Street
San Francisco, California 94111
&
Jossey-Bass Limited
3 Henrietta Street
London WC2E 8LU

Library of Congress Catalogue Card Number LC 73-10943

International Standard Book Number ISBN 0-87589-209-4

Manufactured in the United States of America

JACKET DESIGN BY WILLI BAUM

FIRST EDITION

Code 7403

The Jossey-Bass
Series in Higher Education

JOHN E. ROUECHE, *University of Texas*
Special Advisor, Community and Junior Colleges

Foreword

Planning is an "in" word in education today. It finds its way—along with *accountability, goals and objectives,* and *management by objectives*—into the jargon of most educators as well as of those lay persons involved in education through service on governing boards and commissions, as members of legislatures, or as part of the news media. And yet to date the planning efforts of most educational institutions (and other institutions for that matter) have fallen far short of what society has a right to expect and even demand. Those who have planned colleges will readily admit that they could have done better. The publications available deal primarily with facilities and architectural design and with faculty, programs, students, and finance in an unrelated fashion. Even twenty years ago, having "educational specifications" to hand architects was an innovation.

Dorothy Knoell and Charles McIntyre contend that the need to bring academic, facilities, and fiscal planning together in campus master planning is now critical. They also stress the necessity to regard planning as a continuing process and suggest the use of planning themes as the basis for this process. Such themes can provide the flexibility necessary for reacting to new situations and to new clienteles.

The authors emphasize that community college planning differs from that of most of higher education because of local decision making, responsibility for providing education to the entire community, and concern for what students are like as well as for how many there are. One perfect example is the folly of the concept of "within commuting distance." To have institutions within thirty or forty miles or thirty or forty minutes by paved highway may well be sufficient for senior colleges but not for community colleges since commuting distance for one segment of the community is not the same as that for another.

As a result of such considerations, the concept of a comprehensive community college must give way to the concept of a comprehensive community college education. The authors do not make a case for doing away with college campuses, but they stress that a community college program can be offered with minimal use of campuses as we now know them. Before the campus on the hill becomes the only option considered by board members, administrators, faculty, and the community, planners should explore priorities, goals, needs, the "who," the "why."

Dorothy Knoell and Charles McIntyre offer planners a new, refreshing approach. Their book will add greatly to the professional literature in the community college field. It is needed and will be used.

EDWARD SIMONSEN
Superintendent
Kern Community
College District
(California)

Preface

Community colleges have
changed so much in the last few years that it is now necessary for
planners to consider new options and alternatives to traditional colleges and programs. Plans must be adapted to the declining rate of
enrollment, to the dwindling financial resources for higher education
facilities and programs, to changes in student preferences and
societal needs, to the trend toward placing student financial aid
directly in the hands of students for use at the institutions of their
choice, and to the problems involved when minors are enrolled away
from the district of their parents' residence.

The literature of higher education does not greatly aid the
community college administrator engaged in planning and development; the decisions called for in traditional college and university
planning are different from those faced by community college planners. In the absence of appropriate help in the literature, community
college planning has tended to be stereotyped, with presidents and
governing boards often unwilling to consider alternatives to the
proven model—the medium-sized, suburban campus built on a large
acreage. Planners do not prepare adequately for the decisions they

should make and are poorly informed of the options open to them in each decision area. Furthermore, they tend to be uninformed about the relative payoffs which may be expected from the various options, alone and in combination. There are no (and should not be) standardized formulas to tell the planner-administrator what kind of college he should develop or what specific decisions he should make in doing so. Various planning and decision-making processes can be made explicit, however, in order to provide better decisions.

Resource materials are already available to the planner on facilities, faculty, finance, programs, and projections of enrollments. But little has been written on the process of putting it all together in a comprehensive plan for community colleges at either the local or state level. Academic, facilities, and fiscal planning must be brought together in master planning at all levels. At present, the goal of planning too often is simply provision of the facilities necessary to accommodate projected enrollments within the fiscal capability of the college. Academic and operating budget planning has secondary importance and is sometimes done on only a year-to-year basis. If academic, physical, and fiscal planning are not interrelated in some rational fashion, incorrect decisions are likely to result: buildings may be unsuited to educational programs or instructional technology; incorrect delivery systems may be selected.

Local college planners not only should be concerned with interrelating the various facets of planning, but should attempt to make their plans fit with reasonable consistency into a comprehensive state plan. The simple aggregation of locally developed plans for comprehensive community colleges does not necessarily produce a good state plan for postsecondary education. A good statewide plan should be more than and different from the mere summation of the local plans; it must be predicated on assumptions about the obligation of the state to students. A good state plan should be based on a "back-and-forth" process between the local college and state planners, and regional planners should play an increasing role in the effective provision of access to and utilization of facilities and programs.

Growth in community college enrollments has been so spectacular in recent years that planning has often ignored student needs, characteristics, life styles, and interests. Colleges have limited their planning to the full-time day student who enters college directly from high school with some modicum of skills and motivation for college. The increasing diversity of students requires, however, that realistic options be considered so that all people, without regard to race, sex, place of residence, family background, or prior educational experience, can benefit from postsecondary education. More colleges, more facilities, and more programs will not be enough in the next several decades. Community college planning must include new ways of providing opportunities for lifelong education; and this planning must include continual assessment of its own effectiveness as conditions in the community change.

All community college planning and development efforts can profit significantly from having from the start an explicit set of major themes, articulated as a fundamental planning philosophy. All further planning efforts can be based on those themes. Specific themes will vary from one state to another, among regions of the country, and at various levels of the planning hierarchy—federal, state, regional, and local-institutional. We have developed six themes as the basis for discussion. These themes may not necessarily be relevant for any particular planning group or effort, but they do indicate an approach that can be useful for all kinds and levels of community college planning and development.

1. *The basic nature of community college planning for the next several decades should switch from the facilities emphasis of the sixties to an emphasis on increasing access.* Anticipated demographic changes and attitudes toward public funding will have significant impact upon the character of community college planning during the next several decades. Planning for the sixties emphasized (or should have) efficient allocation of college resources for explosive student growth in a situation of relatively abundant public funds. Now the spectacular growth in student numbers is over. And competing demands for public funds, more conservative attitudes about the role of the public sector, and disruptive events on campuses during the late 1960s and early 1970s have resulted in decreasing public funds for community colleges and all other segments of higher education.

Stable or declining enrollments and relatively scarce public resources dictate that planning efforts be less concerned with developing new permanent campus facilities and more concerned with providing access for students such as the elderly, the disadvantaged, and veterans, who have not previously attended in significant numbers.

2. *The notion of a comprehensive community college should be modified and give way to that of a comprehensive community college education.* Rather than planning around the traditional comprehensive campus, future efforts need to be directed toward a community system for delivering a comprehensive postsecondary education. The traditional campus should become just one part of this system, complemented by other means (such as media) which do not require the continual presence of instructors and also by neighborhood satellites, storefront operations, mobile units, limited-purpose centers, work experience, cooperative education, credit by examination or for previous extracollegiate experience, community library resources, and other community facilities in whatever combination provides access in the most efficient manner.

The community college should become a "contractor," promoting the individual student's objectives by using the campus or community "subcontractors" which best accomplish those objectives. The community college could conceivably operate even without a comprehensive central campus, relying on community library facilities, local firms, public housing—any community resource that is both appropriate and available.

3. *Education should be for multiple adult roles.* The current emphasis on career education obscures the function of community colleges in assisting student performance of other adult roles. Education for the world of work is indisputably a primary community college function, but large segments of the student body are fully trained and experienced in their chosen field of work and seek assistance in improving their effectiveness as householders, consumers, parents, voters, hobbyists, or senior citizens. Indeed most projections of life-style change during the next several decades indicate a probable decrease of nearly one-third in the time an individual devotes to his vocation. Education must increasingly include training for leisure and recreational pursuits.

Young students also need general education for the adult roles they are assuming at an ever earlier age. The lowering of the voting age and the consequent need to establish residence and assume various legal obligations, accompanied by a strong inclination of youth to seek early independence from their families, can be assisted by the community colleges in order to achieve more effective results than what now appear to be taking place without such guidance. Community colleges can offer counseling and guidance, information, work experience, communication-skill development, placement, and follow-up on all these services.

4. *Comprehensive community college education requires more time, more options, and more outcomes.* Planners can no longer assume that community college students are available for full-time, daytime enrollment, continuing until their objectives are achieved. Students are taking more time and trying more options on their way to degrees, certificates, transfer opportunities, or simply a several-course objective which has no explicit measure of completion. Adoption of nonpunative grading policies and allowance for unlimited withdrawals from courses legitimize the exploration of options by community college students who enroll without specific educational or career objectives. "Underprepared" students who attend under open admissions policies also need more time and additional options in order to achieve their objectives.

Students need more time to avail themselves of the many options which community colleges offer; the colleges should in turn evaluate the experiences gained through these options and award credit for those relating to the students' programs of studies and objectives.

5. *Access must be made easy.* Open-door admissions, comprehensive programs, student support services, financial aid, and well-located and sometimes uncrowded facilities are all helpful but do not ensure access to community colleges for all the people whom these institutions are attempting to serve. Both real and imagined barriers systematically exclude certain groups. The distance of the college campus from residences and places of work, the neighborhood in which the campus is located, the costs of attending (the average out-of-pocket cost for attending a tuition-free California community college and living at home has been estimated at seventeen hundred dollars a year), administrative rules (deadlines for compliance with preenrollment requirements and "nuisance" fees),

and mistaken self-perceptions ("I'm not college material") are all access barriers that could be eliminated.

Extraordinary efforts will have to be made by the community colleges, eliciting the cooperation of secondary schools in some instances, if the barriers excluding certain categories of people are to be overcome. Simply being there is not sufficient guarantee of access for all who can profit from postsecondary education.

6. *To be effective, community college planning must be comprehensive; academic, fiscal, and physical planning must be conducted together, and federal, state, and local-institutional planning must be integrated appropriately.* Community college planning has been segmented; academic planning, oriented to the outcomes of student instruction, has been separated from physical, financial, and operating budget planning. More useful planning results when the costs and benefits of partial achievement of academic goals and objectives are conveyed explicitly to policy makers. They then have the opportunity to combine the various plans that previously were devised in an isolated fashion.

Integration of various planning levels may be accomplished by developing a hierarchy of planning themes, goals, and objectives. Once established, this hierarchy provides the basic parameters for all policy and planning decisions. Plans and decisions of each college are then optimal for local purposes but also consistent with state, regional, and national goals for community college education.

In this book, we discuss the concepts of planning and goals, clientele, delivery systems, and programs. We suggest a process in which goals and objectives are established at each level of the decision hierarchy; an iterative process of policy proposal and review then follows which minimizes duplication of decision-making effort. Criteria for analysis and techniques for developing preference rankings for alternative delivery systems are described. We discuss barriers to access in some detail and suggest procedures for defining and studying the characteristics of groups the community college is to serve and then providing alternatives to additional campus facilities and more instructors.

The planning themes run throughout the book, as each is indissolubly related to the others. As we have stated, the specific themes and models may not be relevant to a particular community college planning situation, but the general approach we suggest can be followed. We believe it can be used to much greater effect than the traditional planning systems for postsecondary education.

Thanks are due the Exxon Education Foundation for graciously providing a grant to support research activities undertaken by the junior author in the development of this book.

Sacramento, California
January 1974
Dorothy Knoell
Charles McIntyre

Contents

*Planning
Colleges
for the
Community*

I

Planning in Postsecondary Education

Mr. Z closed another book on planning and said out loud to the four walls of an empty classroom, "But we *have* the new buildings and equipment. I don't need to know how I can build a new facility in a month, I need *students!* How can I add three thousand students in a month? Who'll tell me that?"

Like many other community colleges, Mr. Z's college had more than doubled the number of its students in the previous decade. Planners like Mr. Z had concentrated on adding facilities to accommodate new students. But for the past two years full-time enrollments had not grown, and instead part-time students began to fill the enrollment lists. The part-time students want new and different programs; they want facilities in the community for night courses. Mr. Z's college has facilities that stand unused, and it is still not serving the community. And on top of everything, the college needs more money. The aging buildings cost more to maintain than before, students need costly services, and faculty promotions require salary increases. Where will the money come from?

Mr. Z is just one of the many persons involved in planning and analysis for community colleges who are now caught in dilemmas by the changing nature of the community college student body. He and the others must rework their understanding of the entire planning process, starting at its very roots.

Definitions of the word *planning* range from a simple dictionary analysis—devising or projecting a method or course of action —to more comprehensive descriptions similar to that suggested by P. Drucker (1954, p. 240): "It is the continuous process of making present entrepreneurial (risk-taking) decisions systematically and with the best possible knowledge of their futurity, organizing systematically the efforts needed to carry out these decisions, and measuring results of these decisions against the expectations through organized, systematic feedback."

Planning in post-secondary education (PSE) resembles planning in most any endeavor: it requires value judgments, evaluation and reevaluation of goals, practical assessments and data, and an integration of all of these with each other and among all factors that are affected.

Long-term and short-term policy decisions on the allocation and distribution of resources are the results of the planning process. Two criteria dominate PSE decision-making: resource allocation, and income and opportunity redistribution.

Resource allocation requires an evaluation of benefits attributable to goals or specified objectives. The value of benefits must be compared with the cost of producing them under alternative organization schemes. In PSE identifying and evaluating benefits or objectives is usually termed *educational* or *academic* planning; examination of costs is termed *financial and facilities* planning. Academic and financial and facilities planning have traditionally been conducted as two separate categories, but if correct planning solutions are not to be obtained by accident, they should logically be conducted together.

Carefully developed academic plans that cost too much are

termed *wish lists* by financial planners, who discard the complete plans without appropriate examination of less costly alternatives directed at similar objectives. Academic planners then imagine fiscal constraints which do not exist and develop only those plans and approaches that are "fiscally realistic." The full range of innovative approaches to PSE can thus remain unexplored. More useful planning results when the costs and benefits of semiachieving goals and objectives (called *trade-offs* or *policy alternatives*) are conveyed explicitly to policy makers.

Income and opportunity redistribution must be considered, because it is an invariable result of PSE, even among individuals who do not utilize the services or participate directly in the programs. Planners of PSE usually articulate distribution objectives in terms of providing equal educational opportunities to all individuals regardless of socioeconomic background.

Planning is not completed when criteria evaluation results in policy decisions. Planning must be future-directed and continuous. As G. Lockwood states (1972, p. 414) : "If planning is the collective exercise of foresight, and since foresight is required in most decisions, then planning becomes in practice almost identical with the decision-taking part of management. . . . Planning is the continuous and collective exercise of judgment in the taking of decisions affecting the future." Future plans may be explicit, such as a ten-year master plan for college development or a national study such as "New Students and New Places, Growth of American Higher Education," sponsored by the Carnegie Commission in 1971. Other plans may originate in a current context but nonetheless result in "plans" or judgments about desirable future policies, given current perceptions of future conditions. This type of effort characterized the work of the First National Assembly of the American Association of Community and Junior Colleges, held late in 1972. The topic "Educational Opportunity for All: An Agenda for National Action" arose from the need to order priorities for community in response to inquiries particularly from Congress in its deliberations over the Educational Amendments of 1972. The assembly examined goals and objectives and recommended plans for the future: "In community and junior colleges the beginning point for such an examination [of priorities] is an identification of potential students and their needs. The next step is to plan the services that the colleges will offer in response to those needs" (Yarrington, 1973, p. 6). Future-directed policy recommendations follow.

Policy decisions must be continuously reevaluated in light of changing conditions and changing community tastes and preferences. Plans often set specific time horizons and accompany these by stipulations or assumptions on posthorizon conditions. Planning decisions employ (explicitly or implicitly) a rate-of-time preference, commonly termed *discount rate*. Long-term and short-term policy decisions may be consistent with previous long-term policies, or evolutionary sets of short-term policy decisions can have planned long-term consequences.

Throughout the planning process, numerous separate policy decisions on each facet of PSE should be avoided. If comprehensive central policy direction does not interrelate plans for each area, conflicts and failures are the likely outcomes.

PSE planning should be related to formal elementary and secondary education and all types of informal education as well. Further, PSE planning should interrelate with that of both collegiate (usually termed *degree-granting*) and noncollegiate institutions, and this interrelation should continue among federal, state, regional, and local institutional levels. For example, research activities at universities and colleges may contribute to planning solutions in areas such as land use, transportation, and air quality. Community colleges, as well as four-year PSE institutions, play a major role in the development of manpower for the health and recreation industries, and the research contribution of PSE to the health industry is well known. College planning solutions in such areas need to be consistent with objectives sought by these industries.

Thus the community, whether inner city, rural ghetto, isolated area, or "poor" (in tax base) suburban area, has many needs and problems. These needs and problems are approached from numerous directions with varied policies and tools: regulation and protection, recreation, pollution and waste management, welfare, and dozens of others. Education is only a part of the total solution, and the community college a part of that. The educational needs and preferences of the community must of course be determined if college planning is to be effective. Community college planners must define the function and capability of the college precisely, develop its goals and objectives in that context, and articulate these clearly to the community. Attempts to survey community preferences frequently fail because many citizens are not aware of the educational services the college can and cannot provide because of philosophical or practical reasons. If people in the community understand both the scope and limits of the college, they can make their needs and preferences known within those parameters. The college can then plan accordingly, with a high degree of success.

PSE planning must be extremely future-oriented. With the exception of certain immediate public service activities, research and individual instruction are capital investments; the results of these investments extend over the lifetime of educated individuals. Planning must then encompass long-term considerations of manpower requirements and social conditions, the needs of current students for as much as four decades and perhaps longer. The content of programs and curriculum must be designed around future rather than past life styles. Otherwise the colleges will have to undertake adult retraining programs to a degree far beyond that resulting from normal technological change.

Future planning is speculative, but certain future trends about which there is general consensus provide a basis for planning changes in curricula and programs. H. Kahn and A. J. Weiner suggest (1967) that during the next three decades the work ethic, to which PSE and American society have been oriented, will give way to a "postindustrial" culture in which affluence and leisure continue to increase. In this scenario, society—particularly transportation and communication goods and services—becomes far more complex. By the year 2000, further urbanization results in three megalopolises containing nearly one-half of the population, stretching from Chicago to Pittsburgh, Boston to Washington, and San Francisco to San Diego. Such demographic development emphasizes all of the problems familiar to the urban scene. "Social life becomes more global, complex, and interdependent, the 'system' expands. . . . Personal relationships grow increasingly impersonal rather than intimate: more and more time of people is spent in 'segmental' roles as employees, customers, acquaintances, and bystanders. . . . Communication becomes more instantaneous; travel less time consuming;

and with all these changes, the rate of change itself increases, leading to a need for people to learn to cope with change and 'future shock' " (Hefferlin, 1971, p. 7).

Future trends show a shift by the work force away from private firms to government and nonprofit private groups. Occupations move from primary industries (agriculture, forestry, mining) to secondary industries which process products from primary industries. The most significant movement, however, is to tertiary (service to primary and secondary) and quaternary (those serving tertiary or one another) industries.

During the next decade, the Carnegie Commission (1973) predicts (to no one's surprise) that demand for elementary and secondary teachers will decline due to falling enrollment. For similar demographic reasons, the market for Ph.D.'s, particularly those in humanities who are employed primarily by academic institutions, will be "increasingly unfavorable." Manpower shortages are projected for the health industry, for nurses and allied health workers (categories of particular interest to community colleges). Another significant trend in the labor market results from the efforts of many firms and agencies in affirmative action programs designed to provide equal employment opportunities for racial and ethnic minorities and women.

The average work year is projected to fall from sixteen hundred hours to eleven hundred hours by the year 2000 (Kahn and Wiener, 1967). Life styles for the average individual will shift away from present patterns in which 60 percent of adult life is devoted to a vocation to a possible 40 percent spent on vocation, 40 percent on avocation, and 20 percent on relaxation.

Another aspect of PSE planning involves relatively short-term deployments of resources. This activity (often termed *programing*) deals with selection of appropriate delivery system technologies. In contrast to a number of socialist countries which rely heavily upon planning, American PSE operates on a "laissez-faire" or "free-choice" philosophy. Planning attempts to supply the right amount and kind of education predicted upon existing and anticipated student demand. This emphasis on the general education, collective, nonvocational aspect of PSE was reaffirmed recently by the Carnegie Commission (1973), which also contended that student choices of study fields are highly sensitive to shifts in job markets. While this point is debatable, the egalitarian principle of providing equal opportunities for PSE to all citizens is clear.

The "free-choice" model for planning is questioned when cost savings and efficiency, articulated in terms such as *accountability*, are demanded. Concerns for efficiency may lead to high attrition and difficulty in shifting out of a "mistakenly chosen" program into another, a tendency of concern to community college managers where the "open door" and program and career changes by students are dominant patterns.

In contrast to the free-choice model is the "manpower planning" or "numerous clauses" model (Von Weizsacker, 1972). This model develops projections of manpower needs (usually sponsored by the state), estimates necessary numbers of college graduates to meet these needs, and directs admissions and fee policies to supplying the correct number of graduates. Although this approach appears much more technically efficient than the "free-choice" policy, preferences of potential students play a negligible role. Manpower planning requires reliable forecasts in order to function, and reliability and accuracy of manpower projections are continually under question. Von Weizsacker (1972) argues that the laissez-faire model tends toward the manpower planning model as PSE planning comes under increased scrutiny and criticism.

Whatever the philosophical trends, anticipated demographics and public funding attitudes will have a significant impact upon the character of PSE planning during the next several decades. Planning for the 1960s emphasized (or should have) efficient allocation of college resources for explosive growth, with relatively abundant public resources. Qualified faculty and sufficient facilities were the main problems.

Now explosive growth of PSE appears over. The Carnegie Commission (1971b) anticipates the following enrollment changes: From 1960 to 1970, enrollment increased by 124 percent from the previous decade; from 1970 to 1980, it is expected to increase by 59 percent; then from 1980 to 1990, it is expected to *decrease* by 1 percent; and from 1990 to 2000, it may increase again by 30 percent. Because public funds for PSE are now relatively scarce, planning for the seventies, eighties, and nineties needs to emphasize efficient re-

source allocation for slow growth, or even stable or declining enrollment and relatively scarce resources; the distribution of students
among different types of institutions and programs is now more
important than their numbers.

Student growth rate is, and will continue to be, affected by
increased "stopping out" (where students plan and do return to
school a semester, year, or some other time in the future), pessimism
about PSE effect on job payoff, easing of military draft pressures,
and financial problems. Potential new students for the community
college include high school students, veterans, adults, retired and
elderly persons, culturally and economically disadvantaged persons,
high school dropouts, and career changers, in addition to those who
are normally college bound (Circle, 1973). In dealing with individuals in all these groups, planning may well become more human-
istic, more sophisticated, and hopefully less mechanistic.

Coincidental with the slowed growth and decreased emphasis
on campus facility expansion is an increasing emphasis on cooperative education programs in which community facilities are utilized,
as well as campus facilities. This leads planning from the concept of
a "comprehensive community college" to the concept of a "comprehensive community college education," available to all individuals in
the community who can profit from it. In comprehensive community college education, the traditional comprehensive campus is
just one part, complemented by other means that provide access
efficiently, such as media of all varieties (television, programed self-
study, computer-assisted instruction, and other automated techniques
not requiring the constant presence of faculty), neighborhood
satellites, storefront operations, mobile units, noncomprehensive
college centers, work experience, cooperative education, community
libraries, and other local facilities.

To show how this is accomplished, consider an example of
how a community college can develop a general business curriculum
for formerly employed individuals who desire to upgrade their overall capability and obtain employment. They take courses at the
college center, at a nearby neighborhood satellite, and by television.
Additionally, some are enrolled in a work experience program
sponsored by both the college and a firm and monitored by a supervisor at a prospective place of employment. Several credits may also

be applied to certain assignments that prove knowledge an individual has gained from former job experience. Several courses at a local proprietary business school may be added. The college provides and procures facilities, scheduling, counseling and guidance activity, and thus becomes a "contractor," promoting the individual student's objectives by using the "subcontractors" in the community or on the campus which best accomplish the job. The college could conceivably operate without its own campus, using community library facilities, local firms, and, indeed, any community resource that is both appropriate and available.

Knowledge of the nature of policy-making is important to understand planning. Planners need to examine the numerous political, practical, and personal factors faced by individuals in whom the responsibility for making policy decisions rests. Anticipating alternative future conditions and situations is a difficult and uncertain venture. The longer the time period under consideration, the less confident professional planners can be about outcomes of implementing specific policies. Social conditions and technologies are changing more rapidly than ever; observers predict continued acceleration in the rate of change (Toffler, 1970; Kahn and Wiener, 1967). Planners must participate cautiously, but necessarily, in "informed speculation." The extent of uncertainty, rather than mere risk, must be carefully analyzed, and relevant information must continually be gathered. Thus the choices become restricted, and a clear decision is possible. "It is harder to provide as wide a total range of choice if the unit of choice is large," and "by restricting the number of choices, . . . the information content . . . is reduced" (Tullock, 1969, p. 23).

Two types of error can occur in public policy-making: procedural and substantive (Dror, 1968). Procedural risks come about when obvious decision-making rules are violated or when a decision process is employed that nominally or intuitively displeases constituents. Substantive risks result in a poor allocation of resources, the "real output" of the decision. For policymakers, risk of procedural incorrectness far outweighs risk of substantive error, because substantive error is not generally perceptible to voting constituents or even to board or legislative representatives. Policy results may not be even known completely until those selecting the policy are out of office or have assumed other roles. Legislators or board members are thus unlikely to spend a great deal of time readying themselves for decisions about issues of no concern to constituents and of little or no influence upon subsequent reelection or reappointment.

Another roadblock to effective planning arises from faulty communication. Policymakers who set goals or establish policies are frequently not technical experts in the subject content of their policy area but representatives of the community interests to whom services are directed. Intensive treatment of most any complex area tends to produce considerable unique jargon and method, which may become indecipherable to policymakers. Lay decisionmakers are clearly at a disadvantage unless the professional staff clearly defines the issues and presents policy alternatives in concise, unambiguous, "jargon-free" terms.

"Second-best" or even inappropriate decisions may occur also because the costs of gathering relevant information and developing required analyses exceed the worth of the additional precision in decision-making. Such costs are a part of the planning, programing, and budgeting efforts extolled by many in recent years: (1) assembling "policy-issue knowledge"; (2) constructing a menu of alternatives or courses of action; and, (3) educating the policymaker, so he can interpret and analyze the menu of alternatives and policy-issue information (Dror, 1968).

Policymakers often use decision criteria that are too narrow (leave out relevant factors) or possess inappropriate values (hold views inconsistent with those of constituents). Paradigms constructed by professionals are sometimes technically incorrect, internally inconsistent, or do not correspond to the real issues. Other difficulties in planning are brought about by lack of continuity—one group plans and initiates a major policy for college multimedia, another implements the policy one or two (or more) years later, and a third group, possessing completely different values, follows through and perhaps evaluates the project. This sequence precludes managerial responsibility.

All of the foregoing aberrations in decision-making behavior might be rectified by improved staff work and better selection and organization of decisionmakers. Other departures from apparently best decisions may occur for perfectly rational and unavoidable reasons.

The decisionmaker usually cannot isolate his decisions from his own material and psychological considerations. He cannot avoid considering such things as staying in office, the distribution of income and opportunities among his constituents and others, personal gain, or power—the politics or intangibles of a decision. The decisionmaker selects the policies which maximize his own utility or value, subject to constraints such as his own time, energy, prior knowledge, and available information. The result, therefore, is not always that anticipated by others whose values and constraint sets are different.

Other complexities arise from the act of making the decision. Policymakers and lobbyists may need side payments; they may need to bargain and form coalitions; they have to translate their individual preferences into a group preference consistent with and reflective of constituents' desires; they have to circulate propaganda advertising the merits of the decision. In addition, psychologically some individuals may derive satisfaction from the sheer excitement of decision-making while others detest the pressures of having to make a decision. Finally, problems may arise because intangible and technical skill resources are partially or totally used up while making a decision (Mitchell and Mitchell, 1969). Intangibles, important to the policymaker, include goodwill, prestige, efficacy, and trust. Technical skills, important to the lobbyist, include bargaining ability, persuasiveness, influence, experience, and organization. A technically correct but unpopular decision to set up an innovative college program may destroy the credibility of a policy maker sufficiently that he or she is no longer effective. To counteract this error, the community must be informed more thoroughly about the merits of the proposal.

Theoretically sound solutions to planning and development problems must recognize these practical problems of decision-making if the solutions are to be at all useful. Developing vast quantities of information and extremely sophisticated analyses at considerable cost must be balanced by perceptible improvement in planning decisions. Likewise, significant policymaker and staff effort is wasted on a policy decision of relatively little consequence. Developing information systems and analytical capabilities are activities which, themselves, require college resources and may be quite expensive. Particularly the small and inadequately financed community colleges will find it necessary to identify and direct efforts toward only the most important planning and policy issues. Regional, system-wide, or state-level agencies, due to similar resource problems, must also identify the relative importance of policy issues and identify respective roles in order to avoid excessive duplication of policy-making and planning activities.

Understanding the behavior of decisionmakers is useful to improving community college planning and development. Also essential is an examination of the substance of policy decisions about college operations. Such decisions may be analyzed by the time period encompassed, individuals or units affected, and content and means-ends relationships (Peterson, 1972). Peterson then categorizes decision types as policy, managerial, and operating, which creates a typology analogous to the often cited management cycle of planning, programing, budgeting, (PPB), implementation, and evaluation.

In PPB, planning corresponds to policy decisions which are long term, affect everyone in the college, and deal primarily with ends, goals, and fundamental mission. Policy decisions contain a high value content, rather than factual content (Simon, 1965). They deal with desirable directions rather than specific results, which are not easily measured and which may depend upon the specific values to which decisionmakers adhere.

Managerial decisions correspond to programing and budgeting. They are relatively short term, do not affect everyone at the college, and relate to the allocation of resources among college programs and activities. Programing is the process of examining alternative allocations of college resources to determine which mixes of delivery systems, activities, and programs achieve the college goals and objectives. Budgeting involves pricing resources used in alternative activities and programs, particularly those selected for implementation. There must be a short-term budget for resource appropriation decisions and subsequent fiduciary and program control. PPB systems usually include long-term budget projections (five or ten years) to facilitate planning. Programing and budgeting (managerial) decisions contain less value content and more factual content (objective information) than policy decisions do. Managerial decisions state efficient means to reach the desirable ends stated by policy decisions.

Managerial decisions on programs and delivery systems must be accompanied by periodic or continuous policy decisions supported by "policy analysis." Policy analysis, according to Wildavsky (1969), "requires a high degree of creativity in order to imagine new policies and to test them out without requiring actual experience. Policy analysis calls for the creation of systems in which elements are linked to one another and to operational indicators so that costs and effectiveness of alternatives may be systematically compared. There is no way of knowing in advance whether the analysis will prove intellectually satisfying and politically feasible. Policy analysis is facilitated when (a) goals are easily specified, (b) a large margin of error is allowable, and (c) the cost of the contemplated policy makes large expenditures on analysis worthwhile." Since resources for staff analysis are scarce, most community colleges must identify their most important policy decisions and focus information-gathering and analytical efforts accordingly. For example, greater investment would be justified for decisions on how to accommodate five thousand new students in all programs than for decisions on initiating a new program for training nurses.

The implementation phase of the management cycle, corresponding to operating decisions, handles day-to-day carrying out of programs and activities. These are usually short-term decisions with high fact content and little or no value content, concerned with techniques of implementing means. Operating decisions do have a significant cumulative impact on basic long-range college policy, however. If a faculty is philosophically oriented to lower division transfer education, for example, its orientation can conflict with the overt planning and programing goals of the college, if these goals are to provide general, occupational, and continuing education, as well as serving the transfer function.

Decisions about technical efficiency should be distinguished from those about economic efficiency and equity. *Resources,* or *inputs,* are the labor and capital available to the college in carrying out activities and programs. These resources consist of academic staff, nonacademic staff, expendable equipment and materials, physical plant, and quite importantly, students. Resources must be organized to accomplish desired objectives or carry out stipulated programs. This *activity,* or *function,* of resources includes teaching of English, physical sciences, humanities, life sciences; counseling students; and conducting the library operation, admissions and recordkeeping. Following the resources and their functions is the *output*—the end products. Outputs may include individuals who will subsequently become draftsmen, individuals who are qualified for transfer to a four-year institution to obtain a bachelor's degree in English, and noninstructional programs for the community. Several resources and activities may be combined to produce a single output. For example, to achieve an individual draftsman, drafting courses, "technical vocational courses," and courses in "academic disciplines" will need to be available. In addition, counseling services, the library, and other student services are necessary, to say nothing of the initial admissions and records activities. The contribution of staff services must also be counted.

Both technical and economic efficiency must be related to the broad goal of the college, which is generally to provide equal educational opportunity for everyone in the community. The goal for a specific college will deal with the basic reasons for the existence of that college, for example, providing general education to certain types of individuals, or broad efforts related to veterans, or perhaps enriching the lives of senior citizens in the community. Goals describe the aggregation of end products or college output, the combined results expected from all of the individual programs in the college. At the most general level, goals would define the basic character of the college some five, ten, or fifteen years hence, depending upon the planning horizon.

Objectives are definitive subsets of goals. Measurable (or unmeasurable) objectives may be applied to resources, activities, output, or broad goals. For example, to apply measurable objectives to college resources, one may set a certain date for a certain faculty mix in terms of education and experience. A measurable objective for activities or functions can be the processing of a certain number of individuals in a certain time period through admissions and records. Measurable objectives of output could be the development of a certain number of nurses, draftsmen, or individuals desirous of transfer to specific areas. Relative success in achieving a goal such as enriching lives of the community's elderly might be measured by such specific objectives as the number and geographical locations served and quality of enrichment provided. Objectives can thus provide a measure for both planning and evaluating.

Development of goals and specific objectives forms the basis for a technique known as *management by objectives* (MBO). MBO was first suggested by Drucker (1954) and has since been installed in many private firms. It has been defined as a "continual process whereby superior and subordinate managers of the firm periodically identify its common goals, define each individual's major areas of responsibility in terms of results expected of him, and use these agreed-upon measures as guides for operating each department and for assessing the contribution of each manager to the work of the entire company" (A. Deegan, 1967). As evolved, the approach emphasizes participation on the part of all, explicit formulation of goals and objectives, ongoing evaluation of progress, and the psychological aspects of cooperation between supervisor and subordinate. Numerous articles and books have been written on the use of MBO in community colleges (Lahti, 1971, 1972; Hitt, 1972; Deegan, Gripp, Johnson, and McIntyre, 1974). The major contribution of MBO to planning is the explicit articulation of objectives which then serve to measure the relative achievement of goals (output).

While PPB is based on the practical aspects of economic efficiency, MBO is psychologically based, relying upon motivation and cooperative managerial relationships between superior and subordinate. The two work closely together. MBO specifies working relationships during implementation, provides for policy analysis needed by PPB, and evaluates results of the entire process.

The use of measurable objectives can be applied to economic efficiency. Data on resources can be translated into objects of expenditure. Maintaining data by object not only increases the efficiency of day-to-day operations, but also contributes the necessary information for several critical policy decisions, such as those on salary schedule adjustments, evaluation and selection of teaching methods which involve alternative mixes of employees and equipment, long-term purchasing practices (*inventory policy*), and adjustments to fringe benefits. In addition, resource data provide for analysis of externally imposed price increases for items such as equipment and staff.

Measurement can also be applied to the technical efficiency of resources used in each of the functions or activities of the college. The resource inputs required by a function or activity can be measured and evaluated according to specific objectives of that activity, and alternative arrangements can be continually explored in an effort to increase that efficiency. For example, the resources needed by the registration activity can be either staff or machine equipment or a combination of both. If the objectives of the activity are to process a certain number of students, then the use of resources can be evaluated according to those which process that number of students.

Output must also be measured so that the college is not only technically efficient, but also economically efficient. A community college may be technically efficient at teaching drafting, but if there is no demand for draftsmen in the community, region, or possibly even throughout the state, then the college is not economically efficient. Technical efficiency involves the educational production of the college, but without considering community preference—the need for that educational production—the possible output cannot be measured against the actual output. The most economically efficient situation is that point where the college is producing programs in the most technically efficient manner possible and at the greatest community satisfaction as determined by their preferences. Studies of community educational preferences and future manpower requirements are both difficult and expensive, but they are necessary for optimal decision-making.

Measuring the outputs of community college programs and articulating them in terms of specified objectives is thus not as easy as measuring resources or activities. Program output must be identified and measured by the basic objectives or missions of the community colleges, which are generally to add value to the human capital of specific individuals. The benefits (outputs) accruing solely to the individual are termed *private* while those accruing to all individuals generally are termed *social* or *collective*.

Private benefits are measured by additional lifetime earnings and social and cultural amenities not available to those without college education. Social benefits are less definitive but are thought to include improvements in communication which facilitate political and market processes; reductions in public costs for crime prevention and welfare; increases in civic, charitable, and cultural participation; and improved informal education of children by better educated parents. Since these benefits accrue over the lifetime of a college educated individual, the job of gathering statistics for them requires a longitudinal survey that is totally impractical for decisions in the near future. Indirect or *proxy* measures of college output must therefore be utilized. Such measures concentrate on "value added" in terms of skills and capabilities gained by students undergoing the program. Measures can be made of entrance and persistence rates, college impersonality, class size, student-teacher feedback, self-direction, first employment, or other initial experiences after education.

Numerous attempts at structuring and measuring proxies of final college output have resulted in three categories: (1) general and special development of individual skills and attitudes, most of which are realized after college, (2) immediate benefits accruing to students while enrolled, and (3) immediate benefits accruing to the community. Astin (1972) develops a useful format dichotomizing "student outcomes" into cognitive and affective, each measured by behavioral and psychological data. Whatever output proxies are used, analyses and decisions must recognize that they are proxies—practical but only indirect measures of final output.

Even final outputs of existing college programs are only a part of the community college mission. Although these outputs are measures of technical and economic efficiency, the broader goal of equity is the extension of equal educational opportunity to all individuals in the community. Equality of opportunity cannot be achieved by efficiency, but rather by the removal of barriers to access. Open-door community colleges stress this equality of opportunity by admitting students regardless of age, previous academic performance, income, and location. Consequently, the goal of equity compels considerations of guidance, counseling, remediation, and costs of attendance that are less important to other institutions of higher education.

Equity can only be measured by the extension of opportunity to particular socioeconomic subpopulations of society which have not previously had this opportunity. To measure equity, policy makers have to recognize varying individual needs and preferences and make subjective judgments regarding "who," rather than "how many," or "where" or "when" or "how."

II

Integration of Planning Efforts

Comprehensive state and regional planning and specific local or institutional planning are different but need to be integrated in order for PSE to be effective. Solutions to the problems of planning at these different levels and developing information and analysis require a planning model utilizing an overall hierarchy of goals and objectives that all PSE planners and policymakers can use.

State organization schemes for PSE vary considerably, but most contain established public universities, public liberal arts or "comprehensive" four-year colleges, public two-year community colleges and technical institutes, and private institutions whose character and number vary considerably among states.

The public sector controls about one-half of all institutions classed as collegiate in character, which includes three-fourths of the nine million students enrolled in all collegiate institutions. Perhaps as many as two million more students are enrolled in pro-

19

prietary business, trade, and correspondence schools. In addition, untold numbers of adults are involved in continuing PSE conducted by firms, agencies, and institutions not typically categorized under the rubric of higher education.

The established university enrolls nearly one-third of all students educated in collegiate institutions across the United States. Both public and private colleges enroll 40 percent of all students. Two-year colleges and institutes form the remaining and currently most rapidly growing segment of PSE.

Variations among regions and states consist mostly of the degree of public control. For example, in the New England states of Connecticut, Maine, Massachusettes, New Hampshire, Rhode Island, and Vermont, private institutions enroll nearly 60 percent of all students. Private institutions in the Pacific states of Alaska, California, Hawaii, Nevada, Oregon, and Washington enroll just over 10 percent of all students (Carnegie Commission, 1971b).

In many states the various types of institutions are organized into systems with governing or coordinating boards; in nearly all all states a single state level agency with varying responsibilities is established. The extent of control by these agencies over private institutions varies dramatically. Obviously, nonpublic institutions need to be considered when planning to a degree that depends upon their relative importance in the state.

Planning and problem solving for public higher education are becoming more centralized, partly as an answer to the public quest for "accountability" (Glenny and Hurst, 1971). State agencies are shifting from a coordinating function to a governing function, with an intermediate possibility of a "regulatory" body which has authority to plan and approve policies and programs but no administrative responsibilities. The scheme of relative centralization ranges from voluntary cooperation with a state agency that has no specific legal authority through advisory and regulatory boards with some legal authority to the governing or superboard with pervasive legal authority.

Trends toward centralization are important for the community college, since its orientation, if not its funding, is local. Planning can be determined by where the control of a community college is centralized. Most community colleges are controlled by either the state, a state university, or a combination of state and local control. (See Table 1.)

The fifteen states where community colleges are controlled by a state board of education, which also handles elementary and

Table 1.
TYPES OF COMMUNITY COLLEGE ORGANIZATION

Jurisdiction over Community Colleges	Organization in Charge	Number of States
State	Separate board for community colleges	7
	Board responsible for all PSE	5
State and Local	State board of education	15
	Separate state board for community colleges	6
	State authority responsible for all PSE	7
One or more state universities		10
Vocational-technical institutions		5

Source: Carnegie Commission Report, *Breaking the Access Barriers,* 1971.

NOTE: Some states have more than one arrangement operating.

secondary education, represent the most frequent state-local organization used to provide centralized control of community colleges. The next most frequent organization pattern occurs in ten states where two-year instruction is conducted at university satellite centers, controlled by one or more state universities; this control by the universities constitutes indirect state control.

The relative role of the community college in each state or

region may be described effectively by the proportion of undergraduate students enrolled in community colleges. For example, in California, Florida, Washington, Arizona, Wyoming, and Illinois over one-third of all the undergraduate students are in two-year institutions, whereas Nevada, South Dakota, Maine, New Hampshire, and Montana use other institutions to accommodate lower-division and continuing students.

Numerous organization schemes prevail at the local level. Typically the chief executive officer, whether superintendent, president, or chancellor, is supported by top staff in the areas of student personnel, academic affairs, and operations. As colleges grow in size, other staff assistants appear. Also as districts add campuses, academic and student personnel work at individual colleges, and operating personnel are centralized at the district office. Within the college, an organization of deans, division chairmen, and departmental chairmen reflects the college program.

Many college districts, particularly in urban areas, have several campuses and in some cases numerous satellite centers or storefront operations. This use of the noncomprehensive center should be further developed.

In rural, often isolated communities, community colleges must organize differently. They are small operations which need to minimize fixed costs of administration while presenting a representative menu of programs. Typically, one small comprehensive campus is supplemented by dormitories to house students from beyond effective commuting distance. In addition, adult continuing education centers and perhaps mobile units, such as traveling libraries or demonstration displays, are scattered through the area.

In the suburban area the community college may range from small to a quite large, multicampus operation. Historically, these areas have been characterized by explosive growth in student enrollment but not always in college resources. Some areas will continue to grow, but others will have reached population or student enrollment saturation. Their organization patterns will need to be modified for stable or declining operations.

Where colleges rely on both state and local authorities, usually a local lay decision-making board is elected from the community and allocates funds for programs, determines personnel, initiates or terminates programs, and performs other acts consistent with institutional self-determination. Overall authority is shared to some extent with a state level agency responsible for broad policy, minimum standards, and coordination among institutions. By a recent court decision (the Hadley case), each local college board member is required to represent an equal proportion of those served in the community or within the district boundaries. This one-man-one-vote criterion deals with representation, but the size and character of the service area represented plays an important role too in college planning capabilities. For example, if a seven-person community college board represents a 3.5 million-person community, each board member represents about one-half million people. If the community is heavily industrial, quite large geographically, and extremely diverse in terms of economics, race, and social-cultural attitudes, it might have six comprehensive campuses and nearly a hundred satellite centers. Contrast this with a five-member college board representing a district in which agriculture, forestry, recreation, and related industries constitute the major economic pursuits. The area may be quite large geographically, but its population may total fifty thousand people, ten thousand per board member. One relatively small college and a half-dozen continuing education centers can provide access to a representative group of two-year programs. The difference in individual decision-making in these two examples is obvious: the urban board member (in contrast to the rural board member) represents fifty times the number of constituents, makes policy and perhaps some operating decisions for six times as many colleges and nearly twenty times as many smaller centers, and very likely must comprehend a much more complex and varied set of educational problems. The overall community college goal of satisfying the educational needs and preferences of the community becomes much more difficult for the urban board member, in this instance.

Consider another example where size can conflict with interests. Community college district A contains ten thousand voters. Four thousand favor a bond issue to establish facilities for a comprehensive curriculum and program in the allied health professions; six thousand are opposed. Suppose then, that the district were split into equal units A-1 and A-2. Voters in A-1 favor establishing the health program by a count of three thousand for and two thousand against. The majority in A-2 still oppose the program, by a vote of four thousand against and one thousand in favor. With the two smaller districts, seven out of ten voters got what they wanted, while only six out of ten got what they wanted before the district was divided. And no individual need change his vote on the issue. Thus, the smaller the community college district or service area for which uniform policies are developed, the more likely community educational preferences will be satisfied.

In any case, in spite of huge variations from state to state in two-year college organization and control, planning can and should be conducted so that state, regional, and local interests are all represented. The planning process is determined by *who*—the agents making decisions on various issues, *what*—the substance of issues and problems considered for resolution, and *when*—the proper sequence of decision-making and the time period during which the decision will be effective.

Who includes the state legislature and to a lesser extent the state executive, who set major *pricing* or fee policies for institutions or systems. The colleges in turn set prices by varying the amount of student financial aid distributed. All decision agents determine output or the number and distribution of students educated in the several institutions and colleges: Legislative and executive branches by adopting a broad admissions philosophy, colleges by setting their admissions policies and handling individual cases (counseling and guidance), and students by showing their unique preferences (or lack of them) for certain kinds of colleges and programs.

Contributions by other persons or groups may be formal (legally sanctioned authority by statute, administrative law, or planning documents which carry similar legal force) or informal (authority based on information, expertise, personality, common values and attitudes, or control over social awards). Table 2 shows *who* plans and *what* is each agent's planning domain.

College managers are responsible for operating decisions, some managerial decisions, and a few policy decisions. Many decisions must be made in cognizance of planning by adjacent colleges (interinstitutional decisions). For example, an expensive, possibly low-enrollment allied health program will be better if only one is

Table 2.
PLANNING STRUCTURE

	WHAT: SUBSTANCE OF CONSIDERATION			
	Intra-College	*Inter-Institution*	*Inter-System*	*Public Good or Service*
	College			
WHO: AGENCY		College-system		
			State PSE	
				State fiscal and executive planning branches
				Legislature

developed in a region with cooperative and equitable student interchange. Decisions on other matters and in fact on most operations and managerial concerns are primarily intrainstitutional.

Regional and state concerns are clearly interinstitutional. Table 3 shows the distribution of state sharing; note that three-fourths of the states participate with between 30 and 80 percent of current expenditures and to a somewhat lesser degree for capital outlays in community colleges. State planning criteria should result in distributing resources among colleges so as to assure student access to adequate programs, eliminate unnecessary and undesirable duplication of college programs, and affect an equitable distribution of tax burden among the citizens of the state. Thus the state or regional

Table 3.

DISTRIBUTION OF STATE SHARING OF COMMUNITY COLLEGE
EXPENDITURES, 1967–1968

Percentage	Current Expenditures	Capital Outlay
0	1	6
1–10	1	4
10–20	2	2
20–30	2	2
30–40	12	5
40–50	3	3
50–60	8	3
60–70	5	2
70–80	7	4
80–90	0	1
90–99	1	2
100	1	0
	43	37
No Answer	0	6

Source: Arney, 1971.

authority should be sure that all options have been examined in local efforts and that proposed solutions are the best obtainable in the state and region as well as in the locale.

In the states with separate policy agencies for community colleges, the agencies should direct their attention to the impact of proposals on other educational institutions: elementary, secondary, or higher, and public or private. State agencies may also provide valuable advice in planning methodology, in future estimates such as manpower projections, and in articulating proposals for higher level review. In the states where boards, commissions, or counsels are responsible for all PSE, these bodies need to address intersystem issues, such as articulation of student transfers between two-year and four-year institutions, differentiation of the functions of universities, four-year colleges, and two-year colleges, and allocation of state resources among the systems or institutions. If a new community college campus is proposed, for example, the state PSE agency would be more concerned with the projected distribution of students among the three or four PSE systems in the geographical service area and less concerned with the implications within or among the community colleges of the district. Those implications would be dealt with by a separate policy board for community colleges, if one exists.

PSE contributions by the state finance or budget department and the legislature are somewhat duplicative in all states. This seems appropriate, given the present structure of state governments. These bodies are (or should be) concerned with higher level policy issues dealing with the allocation of state resources among the various goods and services that state produces, regulates, or has produced under contract. The primary concern of the state at this level is the allocation of programs and resources among PSE, elementary and secondary education, recreation, health, welfare, highways, and other public endeavors. Generally, information made available to the legislature is directed almost solely to budgetary matters—the academic planning and programing information necessary to make this fiscal context complete is often missing.

The federal role and potential contribution to community college planning is analogous theoretically to the state role. PSE operations produce external or collective effects that are not locally bounded. For example, individuals in Texas benefit from the community college education of a student in Illinois, particularly if that student moves to Texas sometime after his education is completed. Federal interest in community colleges has grown steadily since the 1963 Manpower Development and Training Act. While not yet completely funded, the Educational Amendments of 1972 suggest major steps for student financial assistance, general aid to institutions, coordinated PSE planning on a statewide basis, and potential funding for developing and expanding community colleges.

Numerous recent decisions by local, state, and federal courts have also had major impact upon college planning. Perhaps the most well-known, *Serrano* v. *Priest* and *Rodriguez* v. *San Antonio Independent School District,* criticized techniques of financing elementary and secondary schools which are similar to techniques of financing community colleges in nearly all states. The courts not only establish broad financial policy decisions by state agencies and colleges, but court decisions on student movement and residency influence student fee and admissions policies.

Major contributors to the planning process, in addition to public and community college administrative staff and policymakers, are of course—community, students, and faculty. Members of the community must be able to state their needs and preferences in the parameters of the college capabilities. Students and faculty must engage in participative planning, particularly as part of certain MBO models. Students contribute primarily in the area of preferred programs and to a lesser extent in the formulation of budgets and other implementation techniques. Faculty should be equipped and encouraged to participate in determining both ends and means. Certainly, they are technically more competent to develop the means than any of the other agents in the planning process. Limited staff resources in most community colleges may be enhanced significantly by the active planning participation of faculty, students, and the community.

What in the planning process—the substance of issues and problems considered—depends on information developed and used by the college and other agencies and the analytical methods employed by planning staff to advise policy makers.

One description of the substance of comprehensive planning includes major decisions about admissions, fees, and statewide organization of public and private postsecondary education (Palola, Lehmann, and Blischke, 1970). The California Master Plan for Higher Education, a long-range plan adopted in 1960, illustrates more details and includes the following topics, among others: structure, function, and coordination; distribution of lower division students; student fees; state scholarships and fellowships; validity of entrance requirements; admissions policies and procedures; retention; enrollment limitations and physical plant needs. Two recent examinations of this plan by the California Coordinating Council for Higher Education and the California Legislature addressed the same issues but placed less emphasis on delineating functions among institutions and more emphasis on new directions for California PSE, such as new and innovative delivery systems, new approaches to student progress, adjusted relationships of PSE and the community and, to a limited extent, possible role of noncollegiate institutions.

The New York Regents Quadrennial Plan for 1972 is similar, beginning with goals for New York PSE through the year 2000 and specific objectives through 1980. Ends and means for strengthening education are discussed and followed by a three-part examination of the population to be served and available resources. A second major division of the plan reviews the specific plans of the state and city universities and private and noncollegiate institutions in New York.

At least nineteen states have prepared master plans under which community colleges have been organized and developed (Hurlburt, 1969). Long-range plans vary from the comprehensive to those dealing with enrollment projections, site selection, budget projections and the like for specific college development. Such specific planning involves a number of "suboptimizing" decisions, given the general philosophies and solutions determined by comprehensive plans. Comprehensive policies regarding tuition and fees, the number and distribution of students to be accommodated, and broad admissions and retention policies for various types of institutions are normally predetermined "givens" for purposes of specific planning efforts.

Policy analysis must be carried on for all types of specific planning problems. Planning that involves specific decisions is initiated and carried on largely at the college level, where most of the basic information for planning is gathered and developed.

Useful information systems should be structured to suit the planning and management style of college analysts and policy makers. Allocating resources to provide information and analysis may be most efficiently accomplished by evaluating the frequency and importance of various policy decisions made by college board members and administrators. If, for example, a college faces twenty major decisions in a typical year, of which fifteen deal with resources and activities while just five deal with programs and goals, the staff should examine establishing an ongoing system which describes both resources and activities. A much more expensive system, accumulating ongoing data on programs, could also be examined, but the infrequency of the decisions, system costs, and difficulty of measuring outputs and specifying program objectives would likely rule out this alternative. If so, program and goal decisions each could be analyzed on an ad hoc study basis.

While this is hypothetical, most major community college decisions appear to fall into the resource-activity area rather than the program-goal area. The most important decision deals with a resource: faculty salary increases. The difference in cost of generating the two types of data is significant. Estimates of system costs are not generally available, but implementing an ongoing program-costing system would probably cost several times that of a resource-activity structure, because of added institutional research requirements.

A resource-activity information system for the hypothetical college both satisfies institutional fiduciary responsibilities and provides for planning and management. Such a structure describes both income and expenditures. For each college activity, data are collected on resources, objects of expenditure, activity measures, and specified objectives for the particular activity. Resources, defined earlier, consist of staff, supplies, materials, equipment, facilities, and students. Objects of expenditure are simply resources with price tags and constitute the basis for determining fiduciary responsibilities. Activity measures, sometimes termed outcomes, provide the basis for measuring internal efficiency. For example, activity measures for instruction include weekly student credit hours, weekly student contact hours, weekly faculty contract hours, number of courses, number of sections, and distribution of classes among major discipline type. Objectives for instructional activities may be articulated in terms of skills, knowledge, and grade credits earned by students. Presumably, different delivery system alternatives would satisfy these objectives to a greater or lesser degree. Such partial satisfaction might be estimated in the planning stage, implemented in the budgeting and management stage, and actual results reviewed in the evaluation stage.

This structure is quite similar to one advocated recently by NCHEMS, the National Center for Higher Education Management Systems (1973), in which program measures are dealt with as resources; financial (objects of expenditure, income); beneficiary groups; target groups; activities; and outcomes. The NCHEMS PCS (Gulko, 1972) is activity-based and follows in large measure the "functions" contained in the College and University Business and Administration (CUBA) Manual. Such structures enjoy widespread use, and future state and federal information requirements will probably be similarly based.

A community college could use its own organization as an activity structure. The English department would constitute the activity described as "teaching of English," and so on. External reporting may need more aggregate data; this is obtained by simple summation for two departments of, say, English and philosophy which combine to form the external reporting activity termed *Letters*. In some situations one or more departments have courses falling into different activity categories for external reporting. For example, if the college biology department conducts courses which fall into both agriculture and natural resources and biological science, numerous difficult prorations of resources in the department need to be made, literally pulling the biology department apart for information purposes.

Numerous planning questions external to the college deal with the differences between the various college functions of general academic, continuing, transfer, and vocational-occupational education. The Taxonomy of HEGIS (Higher Education General Information Survey) dichotomizes college activities between the "conventional academic subdivisions of knowledge and training" and "technological and occupational disciplines leading to associate degrees and other awards below the baccalaureate." This is convenient for states where four-year transfer programs are centered on lower division campuses of the four-year institutions, and vocational-occupational instruction is offered in technical institutes. The HEGIS Taxonomy is less useful, however, in the majority of states with comprehensive community colleges that offer occupational and and transfer education simultaneously, emphasizing counseling in order that the "latent terminal student" (one who enters community college planning to transfer but does not) and others in need of career guidance are not "tracked" into inappropriate academic directions before understanding the range of feasible career options. In this kind of college it is difficult to say whether accounting, secretarial, or marketing courses are "vocational-occupational" or "conventional academic." These courses qualify for funding under the Vocational Education Act of 1968, but at the same time they may have fifteen students enrolled, who have indicated they plan to transfer to a four-year institution and only ten students enrolled who profess to be two-year terminal, preparing for a specific occupation.

One answer to this is a taxonomy for instructional activities or disciplines that is oriented completely by subject matter. Rather than having two categories of accounting, one for vocational-occupational, the other for general academic, just one activity is appropriately assigned to such courses. Courses would thus not be categorized as either terminal or transfer; only the motives or programs undertaken by individual students would be so classified.

Existing taxonomies are also insufficient for purposes of classifying programs or student objectives in the two-year institutions. Furthermore, the plans and course patterns taken by a typical community college student do not often conform to anything in the catalog of the institution. Community college programs should describe students and their actual educational directions, using empirical evidence, for example, "recent high school graduates planning to transfer into hard science programs," "recent high school graduates pursuing two-year programs in allied health occupations," "middle-aged persons pursuing retraining in engineering and related programs," and "elderly citizens involved in general education and cultural (community service) programs." A student-program matrix, such as that in Table 4, may be useful for this purpose. The numbers are hypothetical and categories arbitrary, but represent possible results of assessing a community college district with twenty-five thousand students, several campuses, and numerous satellite centers. Other categories are possible; those listed might be further disaggregated. For example, the seven thousand recent high school graduates in occupational programs might be divided by the thirteen major program types of the U.S. Office of Education Occupational Programs Taxonomy.

Developing information on programs or ad hoc data relative to specific goals may require different cuts through the activity structure. Consider two programs, one designed for recent high school graduates in a two-year allied health occupation, the other for elderly citizens in the fine arts. Staff studies resource use and finds, as expected, the elderly program in fine arts requires more resources

Table 4.
A STUDENT-PROGRAM MATRIX

Programs	Recent High School Graduates	Middle-aged Retrainees	Middle-aged Avocational	Elderly
Transfer	5000	0	0	50
Occupational	7000	4000	100	350
Continuing Education	300	3000	2000	
Community Service	0	900	1200	
Developmental or Remedial	900	50		

from the community service, fine arts, and "noncollege" activities than the allied health program, where most activity requires little or nothing of community service and noncollege activities and facilities. These data require considerable research and study by staff and probably would be developed only for decisions about programs. Goals analysis requires the same approach.

Values for program outcomes or output may be predicated upon those objectives specified during the planning and budgeting stage of MBO. Given the qualitative character of most community college outputs, means other than the usual cost-benefit analysis must be employed.

All information-gathering work must be valid; arbitrary allocations of resource use are worse for decision-making purposes than no allocations at all. Not all costs of institutional support and independent operations can or even should be allocated to each of the programs or goals under analysis. The nature of the particular policy analysis will determine the extent of cost allocation necessary. The decision would need to be of sufficient importance to the college to justify the staff investment to develop the information and analysis. Counter-intuitive conclusions may result from a detailed study.

Using a hypothetical example of three programs labeled A, B, and C illustrates this point. Program A is for students who plan to transfer to four-year institutions and major in a social science; the planners feel that small classes should be used for faculty-student interaction or feedback. Program B is for students learning a trade occupation; considerable work in laboratories and shops is required. Program C is an adult education activity, taught mostly off campus.

Measures of resources and expenditures by program may be developed by identifying instructional, noninstructional, and physical plant resource requirements. Instructional resources are the faculty and supporting staff needed for instruction. NCHEMS suggests an "induced course load matrix," showing the distribution of courses taken by students in these programs. These distributions provide a basis for allocating the expenditures for various instructional activities to each of the three programs. Suppose the instructional expenditures per student per year are calculated to be four hundred dollars in program A, eight hundred dollars in program B, and three hundred dollars in program C.

Noninstructional expenditures must then be calculated. Students in program A use the college library much more heavily and require a great deal more formal counseling and guidance than do those students in B. Program C, on the other hand, requires considerable emphasis on personal counseling and guidance but does not utilize library facilities on campus or require much administrative supervision. Noninstructional expenditures may come to three hundred fifty dollars a year for each student in program A, one hundred fifty for each student in Program B, and three hundred dollars for each student in program C.

The other important resource utilized by these programs is the physical plant. Program A may cost fifty dollars a year per student; program B, four hundred fifty dollars a year; and program C, ten dollars a year. Table 5 shows these expenditures and the totals for each program. The relative expenditures per student for each program are quite different in total than at each of the successive stages; however, limitations of these data are numerous.

The first problem is that decisions are usually made in incremental terms. The figures examined above represent the average costs for the specified period—in this case, one year—for a student in each program. This is quite distinct from the incremental costs incurred when adding a student to each program. Thus if policymakers need

Table 5.
AN EXAMPLE OF EXPENDITURES BY PROGRAM

Type of Expenditure	Program A	B	C
Instructional	$400	$ 800	$300
Noninstructional	350	150	300
Physical plant	50	450	10
Total	$800	$1400	$610

to decide if, given limited resources, it is better to expand program A, B, or C, the decision should be made on the basis of marginal costs and benefits. While program B costs fourteen hundred dollars per student, the cost of adding one or several more students to program B may be less than the costs of adding one or several more students to program A. This might occur if program B incurs its main costs initially and increases costs little as additional students are added to the program; variable costs for program B are then small. Suppose the converse is true for program A; initial or fixed costs are small, and the variable costs of adding students are relatively high. The marginal costs of adding students to A could exceed the costs of B, even though the average cost of B is higher than A. For this kind of decision fixed and variable costs must be well identified. As a rule, much of the instructional costs and a smaller portion of the noninstructional and plant costs will be variable, but this generality may not hold for specific programs.

Suppose policymakers are interested in the cost of developing the average individual to completion of the usual objective in each program, whether this is defined as an A.A. degree, certificate, or simply achievement of a desired capability. Study of student progress and persistence rates reveals that lengths of time for completion of the objectives of each program by the average individual are five and one-half semesters in program A, four semesters in program B, and three semesters in program C. Expenditures per completed student for the three programs are quite different than annual unit expenditures per enrolled student. (See Table 6.)

When analyzed in relation to a proxy measure of output,

Table 6.
EXPENDITURES FOR PROGRAM COMPLETION COMPARED TO
ANNUAL UNIT EXPENDITURES

Program	Total Cost (per completion)	Ratio (to C)	Annual Cost (per enrolled student)	Ratio (to C)
A	2200	2.40	800	1.31
B	2800	3.06	1400	2.30
C	915	1.00	610	1.00

costs for program C decreases while those for program A increases. Data such as that in Table 6 illustrates the relationship between what it costs to conduct programs A, B, and C and the cost of proxy output of each program. Policymakers must be cautious at this juncture. These data do not measure the educational value added to students by each of these programs. Until such measurements are available, either directly or by proxy, conclusions must be drawn very carefully. The policymaker can, however, examine the imputed values of programs A, B, and C and ask, "Are these reasonable in real-world terms?" Even though he cannot measure output or benefits precisely, the policymaker is provided with considerably more insight into implications of allocated resources than he had previously.

Some information not normally generated by the college is required by other agents in the process, in order to increase benefits from more complete communication. NCHEMS, to take one example, has developed a dictionary of data elements for institutions, but has found that additional information is required for statewide planning. "The new sections generally include measures, indicators, etc., of conditions in the state relevant to educational planning and management and also to interactions between educational programs and institutions and other aspects of society in the state" (Wing, 1973). Such dictionaries are useful in developing state-level information systems; greater standardization of terminology would enhance college planning immeasurably. This should not be confused with standardized analyses and planning solutions, both of which are undesirable; greater communication through standardized terminology should encourage the development and adoption of diverse, innovative, and nontraditional planning solutions.

Of equal importance to community college planning is the staff analysis that accompanies information development. The perspective in which past, present, and future college operations are analyzed is critical; information of any character may be expressed in total, average, or marginal (incremental) units. Choice of perspective depends upon the problem; any one or more of the three may be appropriate. But policymakers must keep the distinction in mind. Initial equipment and fixed costs in physics, for example, are extremely expensive. Once these costs are established, however, the variable cost of adding students to the program may be minimal; the size of course sections can be increased, and use of the library, counseling, and other supporting services at the college is minor. In this instance, the average cost for each student may be quite high, while the marginal cost of each additional student is low. As students are added to the program, the impact of the fixed cost becomes less important until marginal and average costs are equal. Policymakers should be interested in marginal costs rather than average or total costs when deciding to expand or contract a particular program, and to do this, both analysts and policymakers have to be able to distinguish between these measures.

Decisions such as those to establish or terminate a program or efforts to achieve broad college goals need to be based on total cost rather than average or marginal cost. Such decisions are based upon multiyear data, requiring use of discount rates to convert results to present value terms. Opportunity costs—the value of putting funds to other uses—must be considered explicitly and tied as closely as possible to measurable objectives. Decisions about relative efficiency of certain college programs or activities, on the other hand, may be based upon average costs and benefits, rather than total or marginal costs.

Numerous analytical techniques are useful to selection of planning solutions, including regression analysis, linear and nonlinear programing, and cost-benefit analysis. Regression analysis is an excellent means of determining the relationship of one variable to another or to several others simultaneously. The general model is expressed as $Y = XB + e$, where, Y is the dependent variable and

X the independent variable(s). B expresses the empirical relationship between the two variables and e the "residual error" or variation in Y that is not explained by X. Thus if B equals three, then an increase of one unit of X results in an increase of three units of Y. If the analyst can predict future values of X with some confidence, he may then apply the regression equation values for B to predict future values of Y. Enrollment, for one example, can be predicted with regression analysis. Students enrolled, the "dependent variable," may be specified as a function of several "independent" variables, including recent high school graduates in the service area, potential continuing students from the previous year, local economic conditions and resulting manpower requirements, changes in college costs and the financial ability of potential students. Quantitative historical relationships are then determined. If these independent variables can be predicted accurately, then the future student enrollment of the college may be derived quantitatively, assuming historical relationships will persist. Regression, however, is helpful in the social science research underlying PSE planning and is used liberally in estimating critical values in many cost simulation models.

Techniques such as taking measures of variances or tests of differences, are not as potent as regression for either explanation or prediction, but if used along with regression, heuristic arguments, informed speculation, intuition, or any other technique that is both valid and useful, they may buttress a more general analytical framework for planning such as linear programing or cost-benefit analysis.

The essence of linear programing is to maximize the value of a set of objectives, given certain technological and organizational constraints on production and a set of available resources. Analysts can then identify the optimal or best solutions under the specified conditions. Linear programing is only occasionally useful, and primarily for rather circumscribed issues, due to the lack of good information regarding the objective set (educational results) and constraints (measures of production activities) and the need to quantify all elements in the exercise.

Cost-benefit (CB) analysis is not as much a tool as an analytical technique that shows which of several alternative proposals is "best," given criteria for selection specified by analysts or policymakers. CB analysis is useful for evaluating alternative community college delivery systems. Among mutually exclusive alternatives, cB analysis seeks to identify the dominant ones by maximizing the difference between benefits and costs. This criterion is preferable to criteria such as ratios of benefits to costs, maximizing benefits, or minimizing costs. Table 7 contrasts problems in using ratios with the use of cB analysis, using a hypothetical study.

Table 7.
AN EXAMPLE OF COST-BENEFIT ANALYSIS

Alternatives	Benefits (B)	Costs (C)	B/C	B–C
a	2	1	2	1
b	5	2	2.5	3
c	7	3	2.3	4
d	8.1	4	2.04	4.1
e	9	5	1.9	4

Five policy alternatives are shown in Table 7. The B/C ratio criterion would result in the selection of alternative *b*, even though it clearly is not the dominant proposal (unless the college is limited to a cost investment of two). The preferred alternative is *d*, where marginal costs nearly equal marginal benefits and the most net benefit is generated (using cB analysis). If resources and costs are fixed, the decision rests on maximizing benefits. If the benefits or outcomes are fixed, minimizing costs is the main concern. Usually, however, decisionmakers find that both costs and benefits vary, and in that case, maximizing the net difference between the two is the desired criterion.

Since most proposals extend beyond one year, values should be discounted for time preference. The arithmetic formula for each alternative is then:

$$\sum_{t=1}^{n} \frac{(B_t - C_t)}{(1 + r)^t}$$

where, B_t = benefits in year t, C_t = costs in year t, r = rate of time preference or discount rate, and n = number of years in the planning horizon; meaning, simply, that the net benefits (benefits less costs) for each year under examination are reduced to "present value" and all are totaled. Discounting to present values for time preference recognizes that benefits are "worth more" next year than, say, twenty years hence; allows for analysis of proposals where costs, benefits, or both vary dramatically from one year to the next; and rules out such irrational alternatives as building a complete campus in one year simply to "beat" anticipated price increases even though resulting facility utilization is low and funds are not available for other highly valued college purposes.

CB analysis cannot be applied directly to analysis of community college policies, but alternative approaches and possible solutions can be determined by examining each problem.

First, costs and benefits are not easily expressed in the unit measure. Costs may be quantified in dollar terms, but for benefits, only the additional lifetime earnings of a student can be reduced to present dollar terms. Other components cannot be measured, and proxies further prevent quantification of benefits. Thus, while the net benefit of a community college alternative cannot be calculated, alternatives under consideration can be ranked in ordinal fashion according to estimated benefits or outcomes for review by decision-makers. The ranking may be based on systematic estimation of the objectives for the alternative considered. Objectives may then act as proxies for output or benefits, since they describe desired outcomes. High or dominant rankings are afforded those alternatives which achieve the greatest number of important objectives.

Quantification of costs lends them greater credibility than is justified, particularly in fiscal planning. But quantitative cost estimates five or ten years in the future are not a great deal more valid than qualitative benefit estimates. The costs are easier to work with, so currently popular simulation models that are useful for long-term projections have been developed for costs, but not for benefits. Theoretically, it is doubtful that the prices applied to college resources accurately reflect opportunity costs of those resources (the value of that resource in its next best use). Such prices are only considered correct, in a theoretical sense, if markets for resources such as faculty are "perfect" (if faculty are paid the value of their contribution to college operations, among other conditions) and if community income is somehow equitably distributed. Neither condition exists in the real world. In a practical sense, though, analysts need not let theoretical price difficulties prevent them from clearly identifying cost differences among policy alternatives.

Once costs are projected and reduced to present value terms, policy alternatives may be ranked from low to high cost to correspond with the benefits rankings. Since the two rankings are based upon different measurements, the trade-offs between high or low cost and high or low output must be imputed subjectively by decisionmakers.

Then analysts must consider planning problems related to the appropriate number of years and discount rate. For a planning model which distinguishes between feasible operating alternatives, ten to fifteen years may be sufficient for a master plan. For most purposes the discount rate ranges between .05 and .20, but the exact level need not be a major concern as long as each alternative is discounted by the same rate.

The most serious deficiency of cb analysis for college decision-making is its neglect of objectives dealing with the extension of educational opportunity. As we have stated previously, criteria associated with this part of the community college mission are not subject to the analytics of economic efficiency but must be considered in terms of somewhat less precise, though nonetheless important, equity conditions, which may be measured by the degree of extension of opportunity. Further, this consideration requires explicit recognition of the varying needs and preferences of individuals. A third set of rankings reflecting an equity criterion could be developed, but it is not possible to combine equity rankings with rankings based upon costs and benefits because it is beyond objective measurement. Staff may present a recommended alternative based upon equity, cost, and benefit rankings, but even the recommendation is subjective and must be examined carefully by policymakers.

Besides the problems inherent in developing information and analysis for planning, related problems may arise in the planning process. Occasionally, several state planning agencies may deliberate upon the same questions and problems. These deliberations may be appropriate in a legal sense, but inappropriate in terms of the contributions to be made by each agent in the decision hierarchy.

While there must be some degree of duplication, each successive decision level should consider more aggregate policy problems, leaving to the preceding level the consideration of more disaggregate problems. For example, state departments of finance often seem to duplicate interinstitutional educational decisions (appropriately made by the single state agency or board for community colleges, or by college districts), whereas decisions of a department of finance seem best confined to considerations about the relative worth of public goods produced by the state.

Another problem concerns the proper sequence of decisions. Consideration of planning proposals by first the state agency and then the agency responsible for just community colleges and then the district planners is not a logical sequence of decision-making responsibility. Lack of proper communication between agents leads to little agreement on the conceptual framework or method of analysis and the factors to be considered at each level. The result may be inconsistent treatment regarding the validity and appropriate aggregation of data. In some states, for example, review methods have been overly concerned with only the criterion of public cost minimization. Consequently, many solutions are likely to be incorrect.

Planning studies are often periodic rather than continuous. Frequent changes in social and economic decisions, revisions to demographic projections, and current and projected changes in college going rates all demand that the planning of community college centers, delivery systems, and district organization should be reexamined continuously.

III

Planning Procedure

We suggest a planning procedure that is an iterative one of proposal, review, and approval within a hierarchy of PSE goals and objectives. The analytical substance of the planning approach consists of two basic criteria: cost-benefit considerations related to the criterion of economic efficiency and a criterion of equity articulated in terms of access or equal opportunity.

Community college planning, whether comprehensive or specific, should take place within an explicit hierarchy of planning themes and goals. This hierarchy provides the basic parameters for all policy and planning decisions and involves all levels—national, state, regional, and college. The themes and goals would be subject to continual revision as developments, new policies, and evaluative studies dictate.

At any level, specific objectives may be developed against which performance may be measured. Goals may be derived vertically or horizontally: a college goal may be developed in concert with a state or national goal, or both, in relation to another goal or to goals of the college. If national, state, and local planning is well articulated in a particular state, goals could be derived vertically. For example, if the state has stipulated the goal of "improving the health of its citizenry," PSE is responsible for the "production of sufficient health manpower to meet labor requirements in the industry." Within PSE, the community colleges work to "increase the number and improve the geographical distribution of allied health practitioners," particularly in nursing. Regional planning may be fostered and monitored by the state agency or tended to by adjacent colleges on a volunteer basis. The expense and occasional low enrollments in many allied health and other programs suggest the desirability of cooperative joint efforts among colleges in intrastate regions, perhaps also in interstate regions. Whether the arrangement is an informal consortia or a more formal joint powers agency, provisions for students, program design, and funding must be explicit.

Development of the goals hierarchy is greatly facilitated by specifying a planning philosophy for community colleges, which aids in communication with all agents in the planning hierarchy. The substance of any themes set may vary from state to state and from level to level. The themes themselves may range from scientifically derived assumptions or informed speculations about future conditions all the way to normative statements of fundamental philosophy about which there is general consensus on the part of the planning agents. Obviously, all agents in the planning process should participate in developing the state planning themes. College themes and goals might involve just the community, college staff, students, and a state representative (for advice and assistance, if necessary).

Planners at an individual community college begin a planning "round" by observing the regional, state, and federal goals and the various planning themes and philosophies, including their own. They then select college goals to fit generally within regional, state, and federal goals. Objectives are then specified, as well as alternative means—programs and activities for meeting the goals and objectives. Policy analysis then provides decisionmakers with the information and analysis to select the most desirable alternatives and make related implementation and budgeting decisions. Budget resources cannot be specified or implementation proceed if the resource parameters are not already specified by a higher level agency. In this case, the decision may be subject to higher level review prior to implementation. Higher level agencies may wish to minimize the number and weight of such approvals so they have more time and ability to stay current with more important issues. If unrestricted state and federal grants are given to community colleges to allocate for themselves, time is saved by higher level agencies.

Staff at all decision levels should reach agreement early in the planning process regarding the fundamental parameters of the problem: the service area of the college, the number and nature of projected students and community individuals to be served, and the range of feasible alternatives to be considered. The planning round should be initiated by the college with the assistance and cooperation of the state agency for community colleges. Ideally, the process would not proceed until that agency and the local district and college come to agreement on the preferred alternative. The college would develop data and analysis with the advice and assistance provided by the state agent. Differing policy concerns of higher level agencies—state agency for PSE, department of finance, and legislature—may require planning models which reflect more aggregate objectives.

During and after implementation each agency from the college on up should evaluate progress in meeting its own goals and review evaluations of lower goals by lower agencies. Evaluations encompass the degree to which goals or ends are met and the relative efficiency of means (primarily at the colleges). Evaluations are then integrated with needs assessment, and goals are reformulated for the next planning round at each level.

The timing of planning rounds varies by level of the planning hierarchy. At the college level, activities and resources are typically analyzed at least annually, perhaps more often during the short-term budget process and catalog development; goals and programs are analyzed less frequently though some may be reviewed annually. The goals and philosophy of a statewide plan should be reexamined annually or nearly that often. National or interstate regional planning rounds for PSE may occur less frequently, though certain planning themes and goals are reviewed each year during the budget process. Timing of planning rounds may vary from state to state. It is more important however that themes, goals, and objectives be up-to-date and communicated expeditiously to all planning agents.

The scheme used for analysis relies upon initial agreement on the analytical approach or model, the variables to be included, and quantification to the extent possible. Where quantification is not possible, shadow values may be imputed or the judgment of decisionmakers utilized. Inclusion of all relevant variables (even if not precisely measured) should produce more nearly correct solutions than if only the variables subject to strict quantification are used.

Policy analysis for college planning proceeds generally according to the following steps: (1) identification of the community or service area and the specific educational need(s) and preference(s) to be serviced by the college; (2) prediction of the number and character of individuals to be served during the period for which the plan is prepared; (3) identification of feasible alternatives for serving individuals; (4) analysis of benefits; (5) analysis of costs; (6) analysis of equity or access; and (7) choice of preferred alternative by decisionmakers.

Identifying the community or service area and the educational needs and preferences of its individuals begins by determining and describing the general socioeconomic character of the individuals. For various socioeconomic subpopulations, analysts consider location, distance and time from college(s), distributions of family and per capita income, parental educational attainment, ethnic composition, educational background of students, and other such variables important in determining possible relationships between individuals and colleges. Other data describing the area are useful and may include topography, public transportation, local economy, general character (urban, suburban, inner-city), and area in square miles.

This "community profile" may be developed in a special study by staff or drawn from existing sources of information external to the college information system. Primary sources of external information include work by local and regional planning commissions, statistics gathered and disseminated by the federal Department of Commerce, and information developed by other public and private agencies. City planning commissions are typically charged by law with zoning and other matters determining city boundaries, modified by incorporation or annexation. Regional commissions frequently serve as clearinghouses for information and may construct regional profiles and possibly also community profiles.

Census data for 1970 provide a complete sample of the color or race, age, sex, and marital status of the head of household and a less complete sampling for numerous other items, including income, education, employment, type of occupation, previous residence, housing units and other housing characteristics. Census reports may not be always useful since the major geographic subdivisions are either too aggregate or do not coincide with the service area of a college. Summary tapes contain data categorized by zip code areas or tracts of approximately four thousand people each from aggregations of appropriate block groups averaging one thousand people or enumeration districts averaging two hundred fifty housing units. Summary tapes can be obtained with data in several groups or groupings. The primary disadvantage to using census data is, of course, its age, but for most planning problems even up-to-date information has limitations, because staff must attempt to anticipate trends in community characteristics.

Assessment of educational needs and preferences of a community may be done on an overall basis or for just a particular issue such as the specific preferences of the elderly. Techniques for needs assessment range from the participative, in which college staff, students, and a large segment of the community are involved, to the relatively nonparticipative, evolutionary approach in which the chief executive or board of trustees articulate the needs they have observed from their experiences. To supplement these perceptions of need, the staff often conducts local or regional industry surveys and utilizes external data sources such as the Department of Commerce, National Association of Manufacturers, Chamber of Commerce, and the various planning agencies and commissions who may assist particularly in providing projections about the future. Survey tools range from the one-shot questionnaire administered to a large sample of the concerned population to the personal interviews of a rather limited group, perhaps selected as representative of the community in general. The Battelle Institute, in its project with the Kellogg Foundation and League for Innovation to develop a participative planning and management model for community colleges, uses a questionnaire survey of college groups representing staff, students, and local community. Each questionnaire lists conditions at the college and asks the extent that each should exist and the extent that it does exist. Need is defined in terms of the difference between what exists and what should exist, as perceived by the seven groups of individuals.

Another supplementary technique is the Delphi Method, first developed by the Rand Corporation. Delphi relies on a panel of experts who are unknown to one another. Panelists' responses to questions are analyzed statistically; controlled feedback about these responses is provided to panelists in successive rounds of questioning. The technique has proved useful in determining the degree of agreement about an uncertain future change or current issue. Anonymity enhances the accuracy of estimates and prevents interpersonal influences. According to Huckfeldt (1972), the response rate, even with a quite large panel of several hundred, may exceed that of most survey methods. The Delphi Method can be more useful in identifying future community conditions than needs and preferences. Whatever the technique used, the combining of needs assessment with specification of goals and objectives provides the best existing solution to the problem of measuring the benefits or output of community colleges.

The second step of policy analysis, prediction of the number and character of individuals to be served, is based upon existing or anticipated planning issues. Generally, however, the college requires information on motive (transfer, occupational, or other), status (first-time, continuing, returning, freshman, sophomore, or the like), attendance patterns (day or evening, full-time or part-time, and terms attended), subjects of program (biological science, physical science, humanities, or perhaps more specific areas such as chemistry, dental hygiene, drafting, or English), and a host of socioeconomic characteristics of students.

The basic problem is to describe or "model" the flow of students into, through, and out of the programs and activities conducted by a college or a set of colleges (if the perspective is regional or statewide). Several methods are basic to nearly all models currently in use. Ratio techniques, particularly *cohort survival* and *class progression,* serve as estimates of the probability that individuals pass from one category to another, such as between class levels from freshman to sophomore or between programs from English to drafting. A related formal mathematical structure, the Markov Process, uses transition probabilities for movements between categories, based on the assumption that such transitions are independent of past events. The process typically involves a matrix of probability estimates for all possible combinations of moves and thus cannot, as a practical matter, be extended too far into the past or future.

Two enrollment models of possible use to colleges are contained in larger planning models. These are the student flow components of CAMPUS, developed by the Systems Research Group of Toronto, and CAP:SC, developed especially for small colleges by Peat Marwick and Mitchell. At the state level, most agencies that have developed or used forecasting methods rely on ratio techniques or combinations of techniques and models; only three of thirty-seven states use gross population or the eighteen to twenty-four-year-old population as a basis for forecasts; just two states indicate use of time series regression (Wing and Tsai, 1972).

For the college planner, it should be possible to estimate transition probabilities according to status, level, and attendance patterns as students progress through the institution. Estimates may be derived from historical data using analytical techniques such as least squares, exponential smoothing, sample means, conjecture, or whatever is appropriate. Required data are readily available from the Admissions and Records Office. Longitudinal data (following the same student over time) are not necessary for this purpose. The more easily collected and stored time-series data are sufficient. More difficult, though still possible to obtain, are data distributing students by type of motive or objectives and certain socioeconomic data.

Describing and estimating the flow into and out of the college is a more difficult task. Numerous factors influence the student's decision to enroll, and students with different backgrounds are known to be influenced differently by the same factor. In general, the relevant variables have to do with (1) characteristics of the student and his family (sex, age, racial and ethnic background, marital status, income, parents' income and occupations, residence, and others), (2) factors under the control of the college (tuition and

fees, financial aids, student recruitment policies, admissions policies
and practices, program and degree requirements, grading and retention policies, and program quotas, if any), (3) factors outside the
control of the college (nearby employment opportunities, nearby
PSE institutions and their admissions policies, pool of applicants,
economic conditions locally and regionally, financial aid administered
by other agencies, weather, and adjacent recreational opportunities).

Second-year enrollment in community colleges is typically
less than one-half of first-year enrollment (Medsker and Tillery,
1971). This so-called lack of persistence must be analyzed in its
component parts. Students leaving may drop out, intending not to
return; stop out, intending to return one or several terms later; be
forced out, due most often to academic performance; transfer to
another institution; or leave to pursue a career, having successfully
completed their desired training. The apparent shift to more frequent stopping out and from full-time enrollment to part-time
enrollment and part-time work is significant and must be anticipated
somehow in forecasts. Most two-year colleges have open admissions
for residents of nearby areas, and, one would expect, might project
enrollments based upon demand rather than capacity as do many
four-year institutions. Open-door admissions, however, may be
accompanied by limitations and capacity constraints for individual
programs, such as individuals delaying enrollment or deciding not to
enroll at all. College policies and programs have obvious impact
upon consequent enrollment; if the college undertakes a recruiting
program designed to increase access, the forecasted number and
characteristics of students would naturally be greater than if no
recruiting were conducted.

Whatever the form of the student flow models used by college
planners, the models should approximate the real world as nearly as
possible, recognize limitations arising from numerous critical assumptions required for certain techniques, include all important variables
that may influence decisions to go to college, use data that are
obtainable without undue investments of staff effort, are credible,
and provide output articulated easily to policymakers.

While state data could be aggregations of estimates of individual colleges, Wing and Tsai's 1972 study shows it seldom
happens. It is nonetheless imperative that the planning process in-

clude an explicit mechanism for staff at all levels to reach agreement on estimates of individuals served by colleges under alternative policies and conditions. Staff agreement should occur early in the process so that analysis may proceed and policy-making take place without the hindrance of eleventh-hour arguments about basic data. Even rational decisionmakers will honestly disagree on preferable policies, but there is little need to compound this problem with avoidable disagreements about facts or information derived from facts by standard estimation techniques.

The third step in policy analysis is the identification of feasible alternatives for serving the needs and individuals already identified. Feasible alternative systems must be programed for delivering community college educational services. College program experts, who are likely to implement such systems, must construct a wide range of alternatives. Feasible alternatives must be relatively small in number. so that decisionmakers can analyze and comprehend them. An infinite number of minor variations on each alternative is possible in most instances, if policymakers wish to examine trade-offs (usually dollars versus results) beyond those presented initially. But to do so in the first presentation of the problem and possible solutions would probably "boggle" the minds of decisionmakers and be counterproductive. Alternatives in the basic analysis need to be sufficiently distinct from one another that their costs and consequences are quite different and issues and trade-offs are clearly defined.

Feasibility is defined either by natural conditions or decisions generally external to the college. Feasibility should not be confused with desirability, which is the purpose of the whole analytical scheme. Feasibility of establishing facilities may be constrained, for example, by state statutes that designate funding strictly for the construction of new permanent facilities rather than for temporary facility rental or lease. As another example, feasible alternatives for delivering educational services to the elderly may be constrained by a financial limit of so-many dollars per year, having been prescribed by the local college board of trustees and indirectly by the higher state agency in its determination of state funding.

While few in number, policy alternatives should be wide in range, limited only by existing technology, unless otherwise constrained by other external factors. For example, district officials considering the general college operating mode for the next decade, should examine not only expansion of existing campuses or new centers of varying sizes, but also innovative and nontraditional methods of providing college services. Such methods may include use of satellite centers, storefront operations, mobile units, significant self-study or independent-study operations, and multimedia approaches of all kinds, using any available community capability, human or otherwise, in addition to the traditional comprehensive college center.

Just as with data projections, all agents in the planning process should agree quite early in the process on the range of alternatives to be examined. Sufficient time is then left for analysis and decision, and higher level agents cannot, too late for informed response, dispute the direction of planning because this or that alternative was not considered.

The fourth step in policy analysis requires explicit consideration of benefits. Not only private and collective benefits accruing from the college education of individuals, but also public or collective benefits not derived from the education of individuals must be considered. These benefits accrue to a community from the mere presence of the educational institution. Those who participate in "community service" programs and use college facilities benefit specifically; all in the vicinity of the college benefit economically and socially. Indirect or proxy measures must be utilized to determine the benefits with long-range implications. Proxy measures concentrate on the notion of "value added," described in terms of the "skills and capabilities" imparted to students undergoing the college program. These proxies have the advantage of being measured during a student's attendance. In addition, other more immediate and transitory proxies may be described.

Relationships of various proxies to final outputs can be based upon whether benefits are enjoyed while students are enrolled (consumption) or enjoyed later as the educated individual pursues his life, interacting with others in society (investment). Consumption benefits include transitory benefits to the student and the community. The student benefits by his immediate experience of interaction with others in an intellectual atmosphere, aesthetics, satisfaction, and varied social relationships, and his personal, social, and economic needs are fulfilled. Transitory benefits of consumption by the community consist of formal programs, informal services, public use of facilities, and attraction of business.

Investment benefits center on the value added to human capital, the personal development of the student. This development is to result in changes in the student's ability to think critically, conceptualize, communicate, and so forth (cognitive), and in his sensitivity, empathy, tolerance, sense of identity, and so forth (affective), from all of which emerges a "whole person." Changes in the student's knowledge and skills result in his being a "specialized person." Both the student and society benefit from this development; the student can attain greater earnings, increased social status, and so forth, and the society benefits from the presence and life of another educated individual. "Whole-person" and "specialized-person" values added to individuals are affected quite differently by different college policies and programs. The "whole-person" outcomes are a prime investment of the public, theoretically, and those are the most difficult to measure.

Many other taxonomies could be used by college planners to specify outcomes. Astin (1972) has developed a taxonomy for other purposes which might be useful in planning. First he divides student outcomes into cognitive and affective, then categorizes each as behavioral or psychological. Thus *cognitive psychological* outcomes include knowledge, general intelligence, critical thinking ability, basic skills, special aptitudes, and academic achievement. *Cognitive behavioral* outcomes are level of educational attainment, and vocational achievements (level of responsibility, income, and awards of special recognition). *Affective psychological* outcomes include self-concept, interests, values, attitudes, beliefs, drive for achievement, and satisfaction with college. And finally, the *affective behavioral* outcomes are choice of a major or career, avocations, mental health, citizenship, and interpersonal relationships.

Most measures for cognitive outcomes and affective behavioral indices are observable. Completions of degrees or certificates, largely four-year indices, are suggested along with daily activities. Affective psychological measures rely primarily upon the perceptions of the individual.

Another taxonomy largely developed for decision-making

purposes is based upon the traditional PSE functions of instruction, research, and public service (Micek and Wallhaus, 1973). The list is similar to Astin's in content, but it is structured on the basis of student growth and development, development of new knowledge and art forms, and community development and service. Student growth and development includes *knowledge and skills development* (knowledge development, skills development, combining knowledge and skills, and attitudes, values, and beliefs); *social development* (social skills and social attitudes, values, and beliefs); *personal development* (student health and student personal attitudes, values, and beliefs); and *career development* (career preparation and career attitudes, values, and beliefs). The development of new knowledge and art forms is not further specified. Community development and service shows in both community development and community service, and in long-term community affects.

Micek and Wallhaus suggest that knowledge be measured by student scores on general and specific segments of tests such as the Scholastic Aptitude Test, College Level Examination Program, and Graduate Record Examination, all developed by the Educational Testing Service. Skills, capabilities, and attitudes are measured by behavior such as participation in political and community activities or from results of applying test instruments such as the Omnibus Personality Inventory, Higher Education Measurement and Evaluation KIT, and a Study of Values Manual (Center for Research and Development in Higher Education, 1962; Center for Study of Evaluation, UCLA, 1971; and Allport, Vernon, and Lindsey, 1960).

All of these measures may be useful in analyzing and evaluating existing or completed efforts, but the community college planner must be careful to distinguish the values of the measures from the desired goals or outcomes of two-year colleges. The tests must be used in a relative or comparative framework measuring the development in a student between two points in time (sometimes termed *testing in and testing out*) or comparing the development of groups of students in different college settings or even different colleges. The measures do not reveal benefits that might have resulted from policies never adopted.

Evaluation may be useful as background information in the

subsequent planning round. The basic problem, however, is to construct a set of *expected* benefits or outcomes from policy alternatives that may be implemented in the future. Comparison between alternatives is more important than comparison between points in time or between colleges. The analytical scheme should result in an ordinal ranking of alternatives according to expected value of each of their benefits. A high degree of subjective judgment must accompany the few objective criteria that may be developed, but the effort is clearly useful if pursued systematically by staff according to ground rules known to and endorsed by college policymakers.

Systematic estimation of benefits or outcomes can begin by recognizing the specific relationship between student-related benefits or outcomes and different policy and program alternatives. Policy and program alternatives lead to both institutional characteristics and student characteristics. We have already described student characteristics. Institutional characteristics include the potential for peer-group contact, student-faculty contact out of class, teaching methods including class size, lecture-discussion orientation and media use, campus environment, adequacy of noninstructional facilities, admissions, grading and retention policies, student personnel services, use of faculty as advisors, and others. Institutional and student characteristics both have an effect on each other and both affect student-related benefits or outcomes.

Six relationships provide a system for identifying and specifying relationships from program and policy alternatives to student-related benefits or outcomes: (1) from alternatives to institutional characteristics; (2) from alternatives to student characteristics; (3) from institutional characteristics to student characteristics; (4) from student characteristics to institutional characteristics; (5) from institutional characteristics to student benefits or outcomes; and (6) from student characteristics to student benefits and outcomes.

Relationships 1 and 2 are fundamental changes brought about by implementing each alternative. For example, alternative A may enhance the potential for peer-group contact (an institutional characteristic) among students both in and out of class (relationship 1), but it may simultaneously reduce the racial and ethnic heterogeneity of the student population (relationship 2). Enhancing peer-group contact may induce a larger and more varied student enrollment (relationship *3*) while the reduced racial and ethnic heterogeneity influences the quality and perhaps quantity of peer-group contact (relationship *4*). Finally, these factors have direct and significant impact on relationships *5* and *6,* specifically the outcomes of whole-person value added, immediate experience of an intellectual atmosphere, social need fulfillment, and the immediate experience of varied social relationships. Changes in peer group contact and racial and ethnic mix of students may have less impact upon other student-related outcomes.

Once the various relationships and their relative significance are specified, benefit profiles may be construced and alternatives ranked. Suppose that benefits are described as *specialized person, whole person, immediate experience, need fulfillment,* and *community benefits.* An example of ranking program alternatives A, B, and C for *specialized person* benefits is shown in Table 8. The benefit profile is then constructed by giving greatest weight to the *direct primary* arrays and least weight to the *no apparent impact* arrays. Examination of potential increases in *specialized person* benefits shows that alternative B is most preferred, A is next, and C is least preferred. The exercise is similar for each of the other benefits. A final benefit profile could appear as in Table 9.

Since no quantitative weighting is to be applied to each specific benefit, the ranking of alternatives in terms of total benefits, is subjective. Though transitory benefits consumed in the present by students are described in two categories (*immediate experience* and *need fulfillment*), these categories should not necessarily receive twice the value attributed to the single category of *whole person* benefits. In Table 9, alternative C is clearly least preferred. The choice between A and B depends upon feelings of staff, students, and community about the various benefits. If the consensus of these groups is that specialized training, need fulfillment, and community benefits are most important, then it is likely that B is chosen. The final ranking, with B most preferred, A next, and C least preferred, may then be compared with the cost and equity rankings.

If characteristic-benefit relationships are different for different groups of students, the procedure may be duplicated for each of several community and potential student groups. The results should

Table 8.

RANKING ALTERNATIVES A, B, AND C ACCORDING TO
"SPECIALIZED PERSON" BENEFITS

Direct and Primary Impact	*Decrease*		*Increase*
Program scope and quality	C	A	B
Teaching method	C	A	B
Direct but Secondary Impact			
Peer-group contact	C	B	A
Student-faculty contact, out of class	A	C	B
Campus and adjacent environment	C	B	A
Indirect Impact			
Noninstructional facilities	C	A	B
Instructional facilities	C	B	A
Size and nature of functional units	B	A	C
Geographic units	C	A	B
No Apparent Impact			
Socioeconomic mix of students	A	C	B
Location of college services	A	C	B

Table 9.

A BENEFIT PROFILE

	Alternatives Preferred		
Area of Benefit	*Most*		*Least*
Specialized Person	B	A	C
Whole Person	A	B	C
Immediate Experience	A	B	C
Need Fulfillment	B	C	A
Community	B	C	A

be relatively similar to those obtained for the entire student body,
but they may not always be the same.

Local or state decisionmakers can use these tables of relationships and rankings compiled by the analysts. In addition, analysts

should describe each of the elements, particularly those based upon subjective scales.

To justify the investment of staff, community, and students in developing these rankings, the policy and planning decision would need to hold considerable significance to the college or college system. A more straightforward and perhaps easier method may be undertaken in conjunction with the process of setting goals and specifying objectives, perhaps as part of an MBO exercise or as a measure for the planning philosophy, goals and objectives established at each level of the planning hierarchy. The selected objectives, with specific elaboration, would form the common yardstick against which each policy alternative is examined. This examination, like the ranking examination, is a before-the-fact estimate of the extent to which each policy alternative will satisfy or partially satisfy each objective.

Policymakers and staff (and hopefully community and students) should agree on the objectives and their relative importance before they analyze alternatives. Suppose the established college goal is "to enable students to get their first two years of higher education at *low cost,* secure in the knowledge that they will be able to transfer smoothly and successfully to a four-year school" (Deegan, Gripp, Johnson, and McIntyre, 1974). The two themes in this goal statement, *low cost* and *smooth and successful transfer* need greater specification for practical use. Possible measurable objectives for transfer are considered first. These objectives would include the percentage of student desiring to transfer who are accepted at the four-year school of their first choice, student feelings of security about transfer, the percentage of students who complete transfer requirements and actually do transfer, the percentage of credit hours accepted by the four-year institution. Another more specific instructional objective could be the percentage of those enrolled beyond the fourth week who achieve minimum specified course objectives—a grade point average of 2.5.

Once a set of perhaps twenty objectives are established, alternatives A, B, and C may be analyzed to determine which is expected to result in the greatest satisfaction. In spite of the necessity for subjective judgment, the process is structured and explicit; each alternative is analyzed against the same set of objectives by the same planners. The relative importance of the twenty objectives must be determined. Each may be of equal importance; changes in institutional and student characteristics may also need to be examined though not in detail. If some alternatives only partially satisfy certain objectives, rankings might show that, of the twenty objectives, 18.5 are expected to be satisfied by alternative B, 16 are expected to be satisfied by A, and 12.3 are expected to be satisfied by C.

Goals and specific objectives for costs and equity (access) may be used the same way as for benefits. Whichever method or combination of methods is used, the desired result is an ordinal list of alternatives ranked on a scale from *most preferred* to *least preferred* according to the objectives or expected outcomes and the analytical technique for ranking agreed to beforehand by policymakers, planning staff, and possibly students and community.

Planning costs are developed from market prices applied to estimates of resources required for college operations. True resource prices should be equal to their opportunity cost or their value in the next best alternative use; this is about the closest college planners can come to deriving resource value.

Marginal, average, and total costs are derived from the concepts of fixed and variable costs. A variable cost is applied to a resource whose quantity may be adjusted or changed during the planning period; a fixed cost is applied to a resource whose quantity cannot be adjusted during the planning period. Whether resources are fixed or variable depends upon the length of the planning period. For the typical one-year operating budget plan, most of the community college physical plant is fixed, as are certain staff. Many staff members, particularly those on part-time or temporary employment, are a variable resource. For the longer five-year or ten-year planning period, most resources are variable except the physical plant and equipment inherited from a previous planning period. Analysts work with the amortization cost of the fixed resource, the portion of its total acquisition cost charged against the planning period.

For example, policy alternative A may require that a community building be acquired and remodeled for two million dollars in the second year of a ten-year planning period. The expected life of the facility is twenty years, and it is amortized on a straight-line basis—the same amount of use each year for the life of the facility.

In this case, 9/20 of the acquisition cost would be attributed to year two of the planning period.

Policy alternative C, for another example, might establish a vocational program utilizing an existing power tool laboratory whose acquisition cost occurred during a previous planning period. While the program uses the lab during a previously unused time of day, such use is estimated to reduce the estimated life of the equipment from fifteen to ten years. The equipment was purchased for thirty thousand dollars five years before and would have been valued at eighteen thousand dollars at the end of planning year one. But the implementation of policy alternative C would result in a twelve thousand-dollar value of the equipment at the end of the same point of time. Thus, the "variable overhead cost" of alternative C is six thousand dollars for the planning period.

The cost of any alternative should be the opportunity cost resulting from its implementation. Opportunity costs consist of current variable costs, variable overhead costs, and fixed overhead costs. Pricing is complex, particularly when plant and equipment costs are not amortized as a part of routine accounting procedures. Also most community college expenditure accounting systems were developed initially to handle fiduciary management responsibilities. Only recently have information systems been directed to planning efforts, but still the collection of certain information is too expensive on a continuing basis and many policy analyses will have to be constructed from ad hoc development of data.

After deriving total, fixed, and variable costs, analysts must categorize marginal and average costs. If programs or policies involve just instruction and not other elements of the college operation (the extreme case), student credit or contact hours would be useful unit or quantity indicators. Other proposals involving both instructional and noninstructional costs and perhaps also community facilities can be put in terms of costs per full-time equivalent student or per head count, making adjustment for the part-time students. Costs per degree or certificates granted are popular in four-year institutions but less useful and possibly misleading for community college planning. Even the cost per completion, with completion defined imaginatively, distorts the CB analysis, since even those failing to complete a program benefit to a certain extent.

Costs may be described as either private or public, just as benefits are. Private costs, the major portion of the total cost, include the value of earnings and leisure a student must forego while he is enrolled and direct costs such as tuition and fees, books, supplies and materials, transportation, additional or perhaps more expensive housing, and any others, which an individual would not incur if he were not a student. Normal costs of room and board and other so-called out-of-pocket living expenses are not costs attributable to community college policies or programs since the individual would incur such expenses even if not enrolled.

Public costs involve activities of instruction and community service and capital expenditures for instructional, supporting, and ancillary facilities.

A third kind of public cost, often borne by the community in general includes increased local tax rates due to removal of potential local tax base, increase in police, fire, and other local services, and implicit costs of the time and effort of community individuals in the promotion of college-related objectives.

The basic objective in estimating costs is to determine how they differ both from one operating alternative to another and from year to year. The private costs of foregone earnings and opportunities may not vary significantly from one alternative to another, although some alternatives may result in varying transportation outlays, parking fees, housing, and extraordinary subsistence.

Some proposals raise private costs while lowering public costs. A prominent example is raising tuition and fees in the absence of public funding. More subtle is the regional planning and location of certain programs that saves college funding by eliminating duplicate, high-cost, low-enrollment programs; private costs may increase if students must commute farther or move. Cost shifts of this kind are distinct from programing alternatives which increase the technical efficiency of the college, decreasing total resources and funding required to turn out a given number of desired outcomes. Private costs may not be altered but public costs may be reduced if increased technical efficiency comes about because of educational technology resulting from new methods, better organization of the college, or increased scale of operating activities.

A change such as slowed growth in enrollment has a direct

impact on estimating costs. As enrollment growth slows, for example, existing buildings age and fewer new buildings are added; costs for maintenance increase proportionately greater than student enrollment increases. Faculty salaries, which constitute nearly eighty percent of current operating costs, increase too. Salaries depend upon changes in salary schedules and movements between various levels on those schedules (termed *merit adjustments*). A rapidly growing college hires large numbers of new staff, generally at low entry levels on the salary schedule. Slowed growth decreases new hires and turnover (due in turn to fewer opportunities elsewhere), and average salaries increase more rapidly even though the salary schedule has not changed.

In planning, costs must be predicted. Most efforts begin by projecting enrollments, applying enrollment-faculty and faculty-supporting staff ratios, and then applying salaries and wages to resulting staff counts. Equipment and facility estimates usually emanate from utilization standards based upon the number and mix of students in various programs. In small colleges, these estimates are usually done by hand, but the available cost simulation models may be more useful. These models generally have a variable multi-year projection component; they are computer driven and eliminate laborious time-consuming hand calculations by quickly estimating the resources required under differing assumptions about operating policies. If college planners decide that it is financially desirable to buy one, there are several to choose from: (1) Comprehensive Analytical Methods for Planning in University Systems (CAMPUS), developed by the Systems Research Group (SRG) in Toronto; (2) Resource Requirements Prediction Model (RRPM), developed by Mathematica for the NCHEMS Project; (3) Computer-Assisted Planning for Small Colleges (CAP:SC), developed by Peat, Marwick, Mitchell, and Company, for an eight-college consortium; (4) Higher Education Long-Range Planning/Planning Translator (HELP/PLANTRAN), developed by the Midwest Research Institute and used by fourteen institutions of the Kansas City Regional Council of Higher Education; and (5) Cost Estimation Model (CEM), developed by NCHEMS for training.

CAMPUS has gone through numerous modifications since it was introduced in 1965. CAMPUS VII may be the most adaptable for a small community college and can be installed using a computer with 16K capacity. CAMPUS VIII, a more complex and disaggregate version, is used by planning and budgeting in the Ontario Community College System, utilizing a large central computer and terminals at each of the twenty colleges. The model provides single-year or multiyear projections of students, faculty, teaching space, supporting staff and space, and financial resources by income type for departments, administrative units, programs, or the entire institution. Installation time requires several weeks plus whatever is required for the college to develop the required data.

The RRPM 1.6, provides output for faculty, supporting staff, and expense, emphasizing average cost per unit for either instructional programs or departments. Like CAMPUS, RRPM 1.6 requires a wide variety of historical data, including a matrix (termed Induced Course Load Matrix) which distributes the course loads taken by students in various programs. The programs may be defined by the college to suit its needs, an advantage for the typical comprehensive community college whose programs are quite unlike the normal four-year programs. Other input information includes faculty-student ratios, assignments, salaries, support staff-faculty ratios, and linear estimating equations or constants for instructional and noninstructional expenses.

CAP:SC and HELP:PLANTRAN were both developed to aid in solution of planning and management problems for consortia of small colleges. HELP:PLANTRAN is not a simulation model; programs are written for computer processing to project, over ten years, the logical consequences of certain important planning elements. The approach is completely flexible but only as precise as the individual programs; it may not relate changes in critical variables as the other models do. CAP:SC or SEARCH, as it is sometimes called, does approach the planning problem by specifying the college as an interactive system. Historical data for students, faculty, programs, facilities, and financial variables are used to project estimates for up to ten years. The level of detail may be varied to suit the individual needs of a college. Variables may be held constant or varied. Course demand is estimated by linear regression.

While these models do provide assistance, the models with student flow components deal only with movement within the college. The user must specify the transformation ratios, with his estimates of future enrollment, and usefully estimating enrollment is perhaps the most difficult task faced by college planners. Further, none of the models deal with private costs, nor are any of them particularly well suited to handle significant anticipated changes in college organization, with nontraditional delivery systems and noncollege facilities.

IV

Analyzing Access

Access to PSE is now a primary concern of educational leaders at the national, state, and local levels. Comprehensive community colleges offer the greatest potential among existing institutions and delivery systems for making PSE available to all without respect to age, sex, race or ethnic group, family income, place of residence, or prior educational experience. But because they are locally controlled, community colleges provide access only to the extent that their local boards establish such goals and adopt appropriate plans to achieve them. The role of the local board is even more important where the colleges are financed to a considerable extent from local tax monies than where community colleges are part of a state or university system. Local community college boards —whether governing or advisory—have primary responsibility for establishing goals and objectives, developing academic and fiscal plans, approving educational policies, and adopting criteria and standards by which they are able to assess the extent to which the colleges are achieving their goals. This responsibility also includes setting priorities and allocating resources for achieving goals and objectives, both annually in connection with budget preparation and the approval of new programs, and over the period of time for master planning.

State and federal governments encourage the expansion of access by policy declarations, broadly stated goals, and financial incentives. But state and federal agencies cannot impose solutions to problems of campus location, types of programs offered, and costs. These problems rest primarily with local governing or advisory boards, who set priorities, make decisions, and allocate resources to expand (or limit) access.

The primary role of the federal government to date has been to encourage the expansion of access in policy declarations by the executive and legislative branches of government and to establish student financial aid programs to reduce the financial barrier to students. (The 1973 funding of the Basic Education Opportunity Grant program makes grants directly to students.) Federal funding has been appropriated to a limited extent for occupational education, facilities, equipment, and libraries. But funds to expand opportunity for groups without adequate access were largely lacking until the Higher Education Amendments of 1972, which authorize general institutional aid for the first time, but only for enrollment of veterans receiving educational assistance or vocational rehabilitation and students receiving various types of federal student financial aid. Congress has previously singled out other groups of students whose enrollment would be "rewarded" with federal aid—students in vocational education, nursing, and other areas of study—but the aid has always been categorical rather than general.

National educational associations make policy declarations about improving access, which are seldom binding on their members but may influence state and local policymakers. The Educational Policies Commission of the National Education Commission (National Education Association, 1964) suggested that as the nation was approaching the goal of universal high school education, its sights should be raised to provide universal opportunity for two additional years of education. The Educational Policies Commission emphasized education for cognitive competencies. Two years later the National Commission on Technology, Automation, and Economic Progress called for "both the theoretical foundation of trade, technical, and business occupations and the opportunity to learn by doing while pursuing liberal education or semiprofessional training" (*Technology and the American Economy,* 1966). In recent years, restatement of this goal by the American Association of Community and Junior Colleges and other higher education associations has become commonplace, with frequent emphasis on the need for access to all who can profit from and are motivated to undertake PSE.

State legislatures and state agencies and governing boards responsible for community colleges adopt policy statements, develop guidelines, and provide financial incentives to improve access to PSE for groups with special needs and problems. State financial incentives include financial aid for low-income students who are unlikely scholarship recipients and for special programs and services to assist variously disadvantaged students who would not succeed in college without such assistance. Minority groups which are seriously underrepresented in higher education have benefited most from special state assistance programs administered by the colleges, although benefits may not legally be limited to racial and ethnic minorities.

State agencies and governing boards have little power to compel locally controlled community colleges to do more than offer on a central campus two-year programs of instruction parallel to those offered by public four-year institutions, with minimum attention to occupational education and no special services to assist students with academic weaknesses. A policy of open admissions means that a college has a responsibility only for developing programs and services which will insure some modicum of success on the part of students with widely differing interests and abilities. Open admissions does not guarantee equal opportunity; this was demonstrated by the admission in the early 1970s of large numbers of minority students with handicaps resulting from poor prior educational experiences. Regional accrediting associations may have a greater influence on community colleges with respect to actual opportunity than state agencies have, because accrediting associations evaluate the outcome of college policies. A college may meet its recruitment goal of increasing its percentages of black students, but if black students show a low persistence rate in the absence of developmental programs or special services, the college may lose its accreditation, which is a more severe penalty than any most state agencies are able (or willing) to impose.

Still, the responsibility for equity of the local community college boards must be emphasized, as the likelihood is slim that a higher authority will compel it to do more. State agencies may even decline to approve programs, courses, facilities, or new campuses proposed by local colleges to expand access in accordance with local perceptions of needs, priorities, and resources. The state agency may also allocate state resources in such a way as to limit the implementation of plans for access which have been developed at the local level.

The strength of the community college as a comprehensive PSE institution rests primarily on its local control and orientation. The best possible roles then for the state agency or board are those of suggesting and encouraging the adoption of goals, providing incentives for the achievement of common goals, reviewing local plans in order to distribute state resources as equitably as possible, and evaluating the aggregated local plans so that if common problems of geographical and program access exist, special state incentives or other actions can be provided.

Special needs for access may also be covered by new types of PSE, either public institutions or extensive public funding. Some community colleges view such institutions as a threat; others, with an elitist orientation, regard the establishment of new institutions as an opportunity to eliminate responsibilities for access which they prefer not to discharge, such as access to vocational education below the technical level or access for minorities who are poorly prepared for college. State and federal funds are becoming available for students to use in nontraditional programs and institutions which have previously been denied funding on the grounds of lack of accreditation; direct aid to institutions enrolling such students may follow. Local community college plans to expand access should take these opportunities into account, since the public may not be willing to support duplicated efforts under these conditions of new access.

Goals for access involve not just people, but also programs and places. Programs must be of interest to the people and assure a reasonable probability of success; programs must be offered at times, places, and under conditions of enrollment which enhance access for the particular groups targeted by the goal. If particular students are recruited to the campus before programs and supporting services are developed to suit their needs and interests, access is not really enhanced. Or if new programs are developed but are offered at times, places, or under circumstances which made it difficult for the potential students to take advantage of them, access is not enhanced, either.

Local policy decisions about access can be limited by state laws and regulations pertaining to functions and programs, including groups to be admitted or excluded, but in most states, local boards have a considerable range of decision-making authority about types of students and programs. College planners must decide first what types of students they wish to attract. An inventory must be made of students currently enrolled—their characteristics, enrollment patterns, and academic and career choices, accompanied by an inventory or profile of the community. Then planners should decide the extent to which their student body should reflect the community, in terms of income level, racial-ethnic identification, place of residence, sex, age, and level of educational attainment. Comparisons of community and college student body will enable planners to identify underrepresented community groups and access problems which cause them to be underrepresented.

The elimination of differences between community and student body do not constitute the college goals for access, but they do provide a point of departure for decisionmakers concerned with improving access. Planners can then proceed to eliminate groups whose needs for PSE are met by other means or those whom state law or regulations prohibit colleges from serving.

With the groups that remain on the list, planners can then assign priorities based on the basic philosophy and goals of the college and the relative need of each group for PSE. If the first priority of the college is to recent high school graduates, planners need only canvass the unmet needs of students in feeder high schools. The first step requires a comparison of the sources of new freshmen at the college with the volume of graduates from local high schools. A list may then be prepared of schools sending fewer than their proportional share of graduates to the community college. High schools with large numbers of graduates participating in other types of PSE should be eliminated from the list. Barriers to enrollment by graduates of the remaining high schools on the list may then be analyzed—distance from the campus, lack of preparation for college, need for financial aid, and lack of orientation to opportunity for PSE. Priorities for setting access goals may then be established, based on relative need of the high school graduates who are underrepresented in the college student body and the means which would be required to remove barriers to their full participation in community college programs.

Besides reducing barriers to enrollment, access goals must insure the success of newly recruited students. This requires a sophisticated approach to defining *success* or *completion*. When the definitions are established, the criteria can be set to measure the achievement of the goal, stated in terms of reducing failure or nonproductive registrations.

Planners must state explicitly the goal, the criteria to measure achievement of the goal, and the standard by which goal achievement will be judged. Thus goals for improved or expanded access should be stated in terms of both the group(s) for whom better access is planned and how access will be improved. Where possible, goals and standards should be stated in terms which permit measurement of both short-term and long-term achievements. If college planners have specified the means for taking all feasible steps to reduce barriers and improve access for certain groups, and if they have explicitly considered and rejected or deferred actions to increase access for other groups, they can use these specifications and considerations to review and update goals, as well as to evaluate progress in the achievement of goals previously adopted.

While they may devote major attention to expanding access, local boards should not cut off access for the students who now have it, particularly those who are working toward baccalaureate degrees. If access becomes diminished for community college students who are qualified and motivated to continue to baccalaureate degrees, the expansion of access to PSE generally will produce new frustrations as well as new opportunities.

Community colleges already do much to lower the major barriers to PSE. College policymakers have usually considered questions of equal opportunities implicitly, if not explicitly, but policy decisions can be improved by a systematic procedure whereby the equity consideration is an explicit part of *every* plan and planning decision.

Analyzing equity of access first requires review of the accessibility of the college to various socioeconomic or ethnic subgroups of the community. Identifying the proportions of potential students from these groups who are admitted and complete specific programs provides information concerning variance of access among these groups. When inequities of access are identified, ways to alleviate or prevent existing constraints and their interaction can be examined.

Subpopulations in the community may be defined with characteristics which are significantly correlated with college attendance rates. The structural properties of the family unit, for example, have an effect on college attendance. Another correlation is based on child spacing (the number of years separating siblings). Adams and Meidam (1968) postulate that within each sex and status category, the individual whose siblings are separated from him by five or more years is more likely to attend college; as the number of years increases, the chance of either or both attending college also increases. Social-psychological dynamics arising from the family's social class position and parents' values and aspirations influence the child's expectations and ambitions regarding PSE, stifling or enhancing his likelihood of attending college. A family's socioeconomic status seems to influence who goes to college, first from an economic perspective and second in terms of the family's values, expectations, ambitions, and aspirations for its offspring.

All these factors correlate significantly with housing. Thus community subgroups may be developed as mutually exclusive geographical areas. Each group is made up of households where individuals exhibit characteristics that are as homogeneous as possible. It is not feasible for the analyst to examine access for each household in the service area, so particular community groups must be held to a number manageable for analysis.

Community groups may be aggregations of the 1970 census tract or block data for population and housing characteristics. Data generated by city, county, and regional planning or other agencies may also be useful. And projections of the possible future characteristics of each subgroup may also be necessary in developing a plan or examining policy alternatives.

The next step is to determine the extent of existing access for each community group selected. District enrollment data should aid in correlating enrollees to local addresses, aggregated by community group. Observations on attendance (full-time or part-time, day or night) as well as the distribution of programs and disciplines taken would then be useful. At this stage, the analyst could identify the constraints within each community group that contribute to above or below average college-going rates.

An obstacle perceived as a barrier by a potential student is a barrier worthy of attention (Ferrin, 1971; Martyn, 1969). Barriers range from the absolute, such as the lack of a college within reasonable traveling time, to the relative effect of cumbersome admissions procedures. Martyn (1969) has categorized barriers as financial, academic, motivational, or geographic (or combinations of these). Financial barriers include both direct and indirect costs to the student such as tuition, fees, books, room and board, clothing, transportation, and foregone income. Academic barriers may arise from poor preparation and low previous performance, in addition to institution-related constraints, such as cultural biases of counselors; the impact of high school counseling, college admissions, financial aid and entrance testing procedures; and the reading levels of the necessary admissions forms (Knoell, 1968). Motivational barriers include peer-group and parental stimulation, recognition of the potential student's past achievements, and the influence of increased ethnic community identity. Geographic barriers include both the distance to campus and the influence on transportation such as weather and area topography.

Other writers using Martyn's approach have examined additional barriers to access. Ferrin (1971) cites the impact of language tests, general education requirements and course prerequisites (within the category of academic barriers) along with psychological obstacles which result from physical distance. Crossland (1971), reviewing minority access, includes many of the barriers already mentioned and discusses the history of racism as the root of all other barriers. Allen (1971) identifies additional barriers to minority group attendance: high pupil-teacher ratios, inharmonious teacher-pupil relationships, lack of available employment and school atmosphere conducive to high aspirations, and conflict in attempts to adapt to both lower-class and middle-class standards. Allen also describes a category of physiological-psychological barriers, including negative stereotypes, poor self-concept, poor diet and health care, and conditioned distrust of whites.

Restructuring the categories of these barriers makes the concepts workable for planning and policy analysis and extends the possibility of programatic or operational solutions. Financial and geographic barriers remain two distinct categories, but academic and motivational barriers are restructured to focus in on individual and institutional barriers. This reordering aids in identifying appropriate solutions. Institutional barriers may be analyzed and ameliorated directly by changing institutional planning and operating policies. Individual constraints can be affected only indirectly by changing institutional policy.

The components of each type of barrier are as follows: (1) *financial barriers:* costs (tuition, fees, books, transportation, room and board, clothing, and personal expenses) and related constraints (foregone personal income, reduced contribution to family support, aversion to borrowing money, and allocation to low-income work); (2) *individual barriers:* motivational constraints (lack of common expectation of college attendance, low parental and peer educational attainment, poor self-concept, lack of recognition of past achievement, inadequate advisement from teachers and counselors, and lack of available employment utilizing high educational attainment), academic constraints (inadequate preparation, low previous performance, low levels of traditionally tested academic aptitude, communication difficulties, and possible culturally based teacher-pupil conflicts), and other individual constraints (likelihood of poor diet and health care, conditioned distrust of whites, and social and psychological distance from home neighborhood to campus setting); (3) *geographic barriers:* physical distance to campus, required travel time, and additional considerations (stress in maintaining schedule, perceived dangers of travel at certain times, perceived distance too great, and weather); (4) *institutional barriers:* enrollment constraints (preadmission testing requirements, rigidity and complexity of admission and financial aid procedures, scheduling of cut-off dates, registration, and financial aid, reading level of instructions and forms, scheduling and financial constraints for fees and books, and adequacy of preadmissions information) and attendance constraints (rigid programs and course prerequisites and requirements, impersonality of instruction, high student-teacher ratios, rigidity of required levels of performance, awkward class scheduling, rigidity of college counseling and guidance, exclusively traditional program and course offerings, and cultural and racial biases of faculty and staff).

The four categories in which potential barriers are grouped interrelate closely and often act together to produce complexes of barriers that resist single solutions. For example, a community college may be located in close proximity to a minority neighborhood, but access is not increased if its programs do not meet the needs of its potential student body or if its administrative procedures tend to be rigid and restrictive. Because of the interrelationships among many of the barriers, efforts to alleviate one will often have secondary effects on others. For instance, if a potential student's motivation to attend were increased, the impact of possible geographic barriers or negative institutional factors might well be reduced. Increased financial aid not only meets the direct cost problem but also can lessen the negative influence of some geographic barriers. If an inequitable campus location were unavoidable, a degree of access could be maintained by increased financial aid for transportation and perhaps additional special programs to help increase motivation and thus offset the negative influences of the location.

Some aspects of the problem are appropriately considered in planning, while other closely related aspects are more operational in nature. Access for specific individuals and groups, not for the community as a whole, concerns college planners. They can then examine the planning and policy alternatives under consideration and see how each alternative relates to the constraints to access.

Suppose that an analysis is conducted to see how alternatives A, B, C, D, and E increase, maintain, or decrease access to community groups a, b, c, d, e, and f. The matrix in Figure 1 summarizes the results of the analysis.

If the access criterion is satisfied if an alternative does not decrease access for any socioeconomic subpopulation, then, using Figure 1, alternatives B, C, and E satisfy the criterion and alternatives A and D do not. Furthermore, each alternative can be ranked according to the number of groups each one increases or

ALTERNATIVES

	A	B	C	D	E
a	↑	↑	↑	↓	↑
b	↑	↑	↑	↑	↑
c	↓	0	↑	↑	0
d	0	↑	↑	0	0
e	↓	0	0	0	↑
f	↑	↑	↑	↑	0

COMMUNITY GROUPS

FIGURE 1. The Effects of Alternatives on Access to Community Groups. Each alternative increases (arrow up), maintains (0), or decreases (arrow down) access for each group.

at least maintains access for. Alternative C is then ranked first, alternative B second, alternative E third, alternative D fourth, and alternative A fifth. This ordinal ranking, while not possessing explicit weight, may be used in conjunction with cost and benefit rankings in the overall analysis.

Community colleges have a clear identity with a community based on geography. For many years, state planners have adopted the goal of establishing community colleges within commuting distance of every resident and have developed statewide plans based on this goal. A number of states—Florida, California, and New York, among others—have achieved the goal, insofar as it is realistic to do so for residents in sparsely populated areas.

While identity with a geographically based service area is essential for community colleges, access is not necessarily provided by having colleges within commuting distance. Community access varies not only according to distance and commuting time, but also in relation to characteristics of populations to be served. For purposes of program planning, planners should define their service areas in terms of potential clients with particular characteristics, only one of which is their place of residence. Access may then be evaluated in terms of the ability of the group members to take advantage of the programs planned for their benefit: are they able to get to the class location for the program? Is the time of day at which the program is offered appropriate to their life style? Are other conditions under which the program is offered harmonious with their needs?

The number of ways in which the potential student population served by comprehensive community colleges may be characterized for purposes of planning is limited only by the scope of the functions espoused by a particular college. One useful clustering of this population is (1) high school students and recent graduates from middle-class or upper-class backgrounds; (2) people up to age twenty-four from low income families, with racial-ethnic minority backgrounds, who may be high school dropouts; (3) employed workers seeking upgrading, retraining, change in occupation, or self-fulfillment through continuing education; (4) women reentering education for self-fulfillment, preparation for employment, or the acquisition of knowledge and skills for improved functioning as adults; (5) retired workers and senior citizens with varying interests in and capability for continuing education; and (6) groups with physical problems of access to the campus, including the physically handicapped, servicemen, veterans, and persons in prisons and mental hospitals.

Middle-class youth will be found throughout the service areas of most colleges. Disadvantaged young people are often in poor high schools with low college-going rates and sometimes minority students in the majority, in poor central city neighborhoods, in public housing projects, and in rural poverty areas. Conditions of poverty and other disadvantagement are likely to be passed on to subsequent generations, in the absence of appropriate opportunity for PSE for young people. The problem of geographical access to campus programs is compounded by the existence of psychological barriers, lack of information about the college, and the diversity of the needs of the group for further education, as well as its financial incapacity to attend even a low-tuition college. The incidence of dropout before high school graduation is high in the group. Many of those who graduate are among the lowest third of all high school graduates, by most traditional measures of academic ability. These are the "new students" whom Cross describes at length in *Beyond the Open Door* (1971), the students for whom community colleges generally have not yet provided suitable opportunities. The correlation between family income level, racial-ethnic backgrounds, and rank on traditional measures of academic ability is high but by no means perfect. Still, young people who rank low on any two of these three measures of disadvantagement warrant attention as a service group of special concern to community colleges.

Community colleges are gaining new vitality as a consequence of their heightened attention to the needs of the local labor force. This group is best characterized by the jobs its members hold and their commitment to continuing education. Few of its members can afford to leave the labor force in order to pursue full-time education; hence the problem of access to programs and courses is complex: when, where, how much, and in what sequence? The size of this service group is virtually limitless. Although they reside throughout the college service area, they may be clustered in certain locations for specific purposes. For example, metropolitan areas will have concentrations of workers in certain large industries, in tracts zoned for small industries, in shopping centers, and in government office buildings—federal, state, county, and local. Still other concentrations are found in labor unions and professional organizations, many of whose members are interested in some type of continuing education for various purposes. The mandate of continuing education as a condition of renewed licensure by the state for many occupations, such as cosmetologists and psychologists, gives additional impetus to community college planners who are concerned with the provision of opportunity for this service group.

Women whose formal education was interrupted for marriage or employment or both constitute another group with whom community college planners should be concerned. Like employed workers, women with needs for continuing education reside in all parts of the college service area but are clustered in ways related to educational planning processes. A few such clusters with particular educational needs are educated women seeking entry or reentry into the labor force; women's organizations for community service or for civic or vocational interests; and mothers of children in child-care or Head Start centers, who may have needs ranging from parent education to job training leading to employment for self-sufficiency. Many community colleges are now mounting special programs for women reentering education or the labor force or both. Some programs are designed specifically for women at or near the poverty level, others for women in the upper middle class who are seeking a new kind of self-fulfillment. Many could profit from ongoing programs, with appropriate educational advisement, but their special problems of access merit attention.

Persons who have retired from the labor force and senior citizens constitute a group which is increasing steadily, as a result of early retirement programs, decisions of individuals to retire early in order to follow new life styles, and greater longevity on the part of all. Clusters of retired persons and their spouses in special residential communities and neighborhood centers may be of particular interest to community colleges which are striving to expand their community service function. Community colleges may also provide programs and services for older adults living on social security or other limited income in central city neighborhoods, to further their non-vocational interests.

Finally, a number of groups exist with special physical problems of access and quite diverse needs and problems, whom community colleges have tended to neglect until recently. The physically handicapped are spread throughout the college service area, often living very marginally as a result of their lack of opportunity for education for employment. Community colleges have a recent awareness of these people and offer financial incentives to make special provisions for them. The problem is to find those who have been neglected for so long, to make them aware of the opportunities offered by the colleges, and to assist them in their entry (or reentry) into education and the labor force.

Servicemen may sometimes be reached by community colleges which use assistance from the American Association of Community and Junior Colleges to establish a special Servicemen's Opportunity College program or which make their own arrangements for extending PSE to servicemen who wish to resume their formal education before discharge. Veterans constitute a special service group primarily because of their special needs and the government benefits which they draw when enrolled. The 1972 Higher Education Amendments made special provision for financial incentives to colleges which increase their percentages of undergraduate students who are receiving veterans educational assistance (or vocational rehabilitation) under a "Veterans' Cost of Instruction Payments" Program.

Institutionalized groups, inmates of prisons and patients in mental hospitals, constitute two additional groups whom community colleges can assist. Both while they are institutionalized and in preparation for their return to their normal life patterns, community colleges can take programs and services to the institutions or obtain limited "study furlough" privileges for the participants.

A community college service area cannot, then, be defined simply as territory encompassed by county or other arbitrary boundaries, nor can access be evaluated in terms of distance from or commuting time to a campus. Instead, for planning purposes access involves the extent to which several special groups are able to avail themselves of PSE opportunities. Planning emphasis in the next decade should be on providing additional access, by taking programs out to where concentrations of potential students are found, and on developing alternative delivery systems which enable students to pursue programs in a nongroup setting.

Community college planners know surprisingly little about potential students. Community colleges for the most part have reached their present stage of growth and development without the benefit of good market research practices involving either potential clientele or college products. One explanation for their phenomenal success lies in the sheer numbers of persons from which the colleges might draw their enrollments. But if the colleges are to achieve further growth in enrollments and to maintain at least their current levels of full-time equivalent students, they must know potential students better.

Professional market surveys for which community colleges might contract are of less potential value under most circumstances than a number of survey techniques and community analyses which community college planning and development staff can undertake without special training, on a continuing or periodically recurring basis. Some of the possible procedures involve a kind of action research in which students, faculty, and staff can all participate on a voluntary basis. Research by college personnel gives them an opportunity for face-to-face encounter with members of the noncollege community, in a nonthreatening situation, from which they can learn about both potential and past students. Other procedures involve the analysis of demographic data collected for other purposes, in which are no direct contacts with the community. Community colleges have surprisingly little data concerning the graduates (or dropouts) of local high schools. Community college staff members know the numbers of new students entering from feeder high schools each year, which are used in projecting future enrollments, but they lack information about college-going rates for all the high schools. Recruitment efforts (which may be little more than the dissemination of information) are then directed toward the feeder high schools, while tending to ignore the others. Because of the recruitment effort and peer influence increasing numbers of students from the feeder high schools come to the college. High schools which were sending few students on to community college experience no growth in college rates as a result of neglect by the community college and the lack of peer influence. The exceptions are high schools serving relatively high-income families; graduates from these schools are more likely to attend residential four-year institutions than community colleges.

College staff needs to identify local high schools with low rates of attendance at any type of PSE institution, inform students in these high schools about opportunities offered by community colleges, and assist those who are interested. First, the community college staff should work with staff at both public and private secondary schools to develop a system for verifying college attendance by members of the graduating class each year and for analyzing college attendance rates by type of institution and by sex, academic ability, socioeconomic status, and racial-ethnic origin of the student. Community college can then focus its efforts on young people who do not yet have an appropriate opportunity for PSE, by providing them with information about current programs and access routes open to them and by upgrading its own response to the needs of the "new student" in higher education.

The second aspect of the high school study involves identifying high school seniors with no plans for PSE, and conducting interviews with those who express interest during a brief information-screening session. Community college students may be employed under the College Work-Study program or recruited as volunteers to serve as interviewers with these high school seniors, individually and in small groups. Special kits of college materials may be prepared for training interviewers, including throwaways to be given to interviewees. The task of the community college interviewers is twofold—to gather information about the students identified as noncollege-attenders and to act as a reference for those who are interested in attending the college as a result of the interview. Secondarily the interviewers act as public relations officers for their colleges. Student interviewers are able to obtain and record information about the high school seniors' plans for the immediate and long-term futures, career interests, expectations about need for further education, perceptions about past educational experiences, and personal characteristics, including family backgrounds. Student interviewers may be selected whose socioeconomic and racial-ethnic backgrounds or common occupational interests suggest rapport with the interviewees.

Data thus obtained may be less objective than those which experienced interviewers would obtain, but if student interviewers relate well to interviewees, they perform both recruitment and public relations functions, while obtaining information useful for plans to expand and extend educational opportunity to groups not now served. Research interest is strongest toward young people from low-income families who may be further disadvantaged by minority-group status or low demonstrated academic ability or both, but middle-class youth from families without a college-going tradition or with negative attitudes toward higher education will also benefit from this type of action research.

Finally, community colleges need to examine the high school origins of their new students who come from nonlocal high schools. Community college students can be quite mobile, because of increased financial aid that makes interstate migration possible, the lowering of the age of majority that permits students to move between districts often without financial aid, and continuing efforts to increase the enrollment of minority students. If community college planners examine the high school origins of their new students periodically, they may gain better understanding of students' educational experiences, motivation, and interests.

Research has been conducted to study high school seniors without plans for college. One research venture interviewed samples of high school seniors and their parents in seven major cities in New York State. Schools were selected on the basis of large concentrations of students who were not college-bound because of economic disadvantage, type of program followed in high school, or both (Knoell, 1966). This study constituted one aspect of a major inquiry into the unmet PSE needs of urban disadvantaged youth; emphasis was placed on how the public two-year colleges could change to meet these needs. Graduate students in education and the social sciences were employed as interviewers in most of the cities, with no local community college involvement. The interview schedule included a series of questions pertaining to the local community college, however, with the objective of finding out whether the subjects were aware of opportunities offered locally, and what perceptions they had of the student body, costs, and programs offered.

Another study of high school seniors was conducted in five large cities in four states, with the objectives of obtaining college attendance rates for black and white high school graduates by sex, ability, and socioeconomic status and to examine the extent to which black graduates, in comparison to white graduates in the same city, are availing themselves of opportunities offered by the local community college (Knoell, 1970). College attendance rates were analyzed so that the colleges could use the findings in establishing priorities and strategies for recruiting black students. Matrices were constructed to show concentrations of non-attenders at various levels of ability and with differing family backgrounds. Data were obtained from a sample of about sixty high schools, to produce a range in racial composition. Approximately equal sized samples of black and white graduates were obtained, less than half of whom went on to college immediately following high school graduation.

The interviews with black students in each city who did not expect to go to college after high school graduation, and who had made no plans to do so, were conducted largely by black students and staff in the local community colleges, who were trained in the use of the interview schedule by qualified research staff members at the colleges. Interviewees were invited to return for a half day of testing, using an experimental, nontraditional battery of instruments;

they were paid a modest fee for both interviews and testing. They were asked (1) how they felt about their high school experiences, (2) what expectation they had of need for further education or training, collegiate or otherwise, (3) what job interests they had developed (types of jobs, job situations, and areas of employment), (4) why they were not going to college and under what conditions they would be interested in doing so, (5) how their families felt about education and the world of work, and (6) what their attitude was toward military service and its training opportunities. Information about family characteristics believed to be related to decision-making about education and jobs was also collected.

The findings from the two studies are less important to particular community colleges than the processes by which they were reached. Each college needs to mount its own studies of the local high schools, from which it can learn how others perceive the college, where concentrations of students remain who might be recruited, what inequalities exist with respect to race, sex, high school attended, and family income, and what changes the college can make to increase educational opportunity for groups not yet fully served.

Census data is another useful means of determining group characteristics of the enrolled students and the communities from which they come. The 1970 national census provides summary data on socioeconomic, educational, occupational, and personal characteristics of residents of census tracts. The residence of new students may be plotted by census tract, which may then be aggregated to describe the college-attendance patterns of students in various sections of the service area which differ widely with respect to the background characteristics of the residents. Furthermore, a kind of demographic map can be constructed for the college district or service area, on which income and educational levels can be depicted to pinpoint areas where residents do not appear to have realistic access to the community college campus or programs.

The Ford Foundation funded a study using 1960 census data to compare rates of college attendance by black and white youth and develop an index of socioeconomic status (Knoell, 1970). The census tract in which each subject resided was identified, and all accumulated tracts were arrayed in terms of the median family income in the 1960 census. Four levels of median income formed workable groupings. Adjustments were made to allow for major changes that had occurred since the 1960 census in the nature of the residential population, for example, redevelopment resulting in middle-income housing. Adjustments were also made to classifications of individuals when information in the school records appeared to invalidate the index based on residence, for example, parental occupation as gardener with the family residing in the highest income area. Time limitations made it impossible to use more than a measure of family income in developing the index of socioeconomic status for the tracts, but even this one measure yielded far greater variance than was needed. Grouping the tracts into very large categories appeared to increase the reliability of the ranks assigned individuals on the basis of only one measure.

Certain individuals were undoubtedly misclassified with respect to socioeconomic status, based on their residence in a census tract having certain characteristics. Nonetheless the technique has a number of advantages over the more traditional means of categorizing students with respect to socioeconomic status. No direct contact with the student is required, in which information is sought about family income, father's occupation, educational level of parents, and other measures used customarily to derive the desired index. For lower class students, group characteristics describing their neighborhoods are often a more reliable index than individual characteristics because of a high incidence of unstable unemployment, absence of the father from the family, and a general lack of information about family characteristics. A large percentage of community college students are adults whose socioeconomic backgrounds may be quite different from those of their parents; however, questionnaires seeking family income and related data seldom differentiate between young students for whom parental information may be relevant and adults who are independent of their families.

Use of census tract data to classify community college students is obviously limited to research and planning purposes, where errors in classification will not penalize the student. Data can be worked up from census tapes to enable college planners to understand both their communities and their students better. Colleges using such data have not yet had sufficient experience to be able to make a recommendation concerning the most useful level of aggregation of census data; aggregation by zip code area, tract, block group, and enumeration district are all available on tapes. The level of aggregation can be judged by the size of the variance in the characteristics which a particular level produces and the size and seriousness of the errors in classification of individuals and neighborhoods produced by zip code area or tract data. As college staff finds recurring uses for census data for their service areas, they may find it worthwhile to work with block or enumeration district data which can be updated as changes occur in the community.

Another type of study, a house-to-house canvass using a standardized interview schedule, will produce desired information about the characteristics and interests of the labor force, women reentering education, senior citizens, and young people from low income areas who are not in school. Census tract data may be used to identify concentrations of low-income families, minorities, various types and levels of workers, persons with less than high school education, and the elderly. Colleges considering special programs for women may also use census data as a means of pinpointing concentrations of women in certain age, education, and income groups.

Three general lines of questioning appear to be useful in providing data for community college planning. The first concerns the interests of interviewees and members of their families in various types and levels of programs which the community college might offer. If subjects express interests, the second set of questions involves the conditions under which they would be likely to enroll in programs—location, time of day, duration, and costs. Finally, answers to certain questions about personal characteristics are needed, in order to be able to categorize the findings by group, for use in specific planning by the college. Personal characteristics data of interest are sex, age, highest level of education attained, occupation, income level, and racial-ethnic background, with others to be added as needed in the particular planning situations. Much information can be obtained by observation; other data requires questions directly to the subject.

One of the broadest surveys to be made, in terms of geographical coverage, was conducted in northeastern California by the Diridon Research Corporation (1972) for the California Coordinating Council for Higher Education and the California Rural Con-

sortium, involving six community colleges in eight counties (Coordinating Council for Higher Education, 1972). A house-to-house
survey instrument was used to obtain basic data, supplemented by a
"decisionmaker" questionnaire used to survey the attitudes of persons who were regarded as important in shaping community opinion
on issues. The general purpose of the study was to survey attitudes
toward and interest in higher and continuing education in northeastern California, as a step in improving PSE opportunities offered
by both the community colleges and the two public senior systems of
higher education. In the house-to-house canvass, questions included
the interviewee's general interest in attending college, problems pre-
venting him from doing so, interest in home instruction, possible
educational objectives to be pursued, and areas of occupational
educational interest, personal interest (such as consumer education,
general cultural improvement), and interest in a major field of
study in a part-time degree program. Questions were also asked concerning personal characteristics, for use in interpreting the attitudinal
and interests data. The survey instrument directed to the sample of
"decisionmakers" also included questions on excesses and shortages
of labor in the local community, in a range of fields and levels of
work, and the fields in which they saw a community need for vocational or career training. Finally, they were asked whether community college offerings in occupational education should be based
on student interest, needs of the local community, or the national
job market.

A large urban community college in an eastern state also
conducted a house-by-house canvass to find out about the community
which it was not serving. Public school officials compiled citywide
rosters of high school seniors who had made no plans to attend
college or to obtain other training. The community college obtained
volunteer interviewers from women in one of the college programs
of training women for "New Careers" in the human services. The
volunteers were instructed in the rudiments of survey techniques,
briefed on the many programs and services offered by the college,
and then dispatched to their own neighborhoods to contact an
assigned list of students from the roster and their families. The
interviewers were given materials describing the college to leave in
the households they visited and were instructed in follow-up procedures for persons expressing interest in enrolling. The interviewers,

for the most part women with low income or on welfare who were proud of their status as students, brought considerable creditability to their household interviews. The primary objective of the study was to arouse interest among families of young people not attending college and to recruit students of all ages from these families. A modicum of success was achieved in reaching this objective, while the study also provided useful feedback to the college concerning its problems in communicating with some parts of its community.

Another study can be directed to part-time students, usually adults who must give lower priority to their educational pursuits than to employment or family responsibilities. Little is known about their objectives, their intentions with respect to persistence, their needs for counseling and other supportive services, or the extent to which the community college is responding satisfactorily to their needs. Colleges are reluctant to probe this area, for fear of discouraging adults from enrolling by the use of questionnaires or interview schedules. The open-door philosophy of the community college is practiced perhaps best in its operation of the adult and continuing education programs, where prospective enrollees must present few or no credentials as a condition of registration. This "free access" for adults to community college programs has the advantage of eliminating the admissions procedures which adults find tiresome—lengthy application forms to be filled out, high school and college transcripts to be submitted, even placement examinations. But the major disadvantage of this "free access" is the resulting total lack of any information about the enrollees to use for either planning or evaluation.

The rate of turnover in enrollments in adult and part-time programs is reputed to be as high as 50 percent each semester, although an undetermined portion of the students are simply "stopouts" for one or more semesters. Still others may have achieved their objectives in one or two semesters, if the objectives were limited to refreshing their conversational French in anticipation of a trip to Europe, brushing up on shorthand skills before reentering employment, or such. In addition to the house-to-house canvass to find out about community interests and needs not being met by the college, a canvass might be made of adult part-time students who appear to be one-time enrollees (they do not enroll in the next regular session following their first-time participation in a college program). The major lines of questioning, which can be done by telephone, in personal interview, or by mailed questionnaire, are (1) what educational, occupational, and personal objectives the person had when he enrolled in the course or program, (2) to what extent the course or program satisfied the objective(s) (or what changes in objective, if any, took place during or as a result of the experience), (3) if withdrawal took place before the end of the term, what circumstances were associated with the decision to withdraw, and was his objective achieved before withdrawal, (4) if the enrollment experience resulted in any demonstrable gain to the individual, such as job promotion or salary increase, (5) if credit earned, and if so, for what purpose it will be used, and (6) if he has any expectation of (or interest in) enrolling again at a later date and what the college could do (more or differently) to facilitate the achievement of his objectives.

Colleges canvassing their former adult part-time enrollees will also want to obtain a limited amount of basic demographic data from the subjects queried, in order to develop a context for interpreting the responses concerning objectives and experiences. The minimum data requirements should include the subjects' age, sex, racial-ethnic identification, prior educational attainment, occupation, income level, and major nonvocational pursuits. Inquiry may also be made into the geographical origins of the subjects (length of residency in the college service area and prior residence in the state or elsewhere) and their family backgrounds (marital status, children, or siblings under eighteen years of age).

A canvass by community colleges of their nonpersisting adult students should serve a threefold purpose. The first is to provide feedback information for use in planning future programs and services for adult part-time students. Feedback should include information about both the course or program completed by the student and his expectations about subsequent enrollment. The canvass should also yield material which can be used to develop a more defensible taxonomy of outcomes for programs for adults than is presently in use at most colleges. Finally, the canvass can serve a useful public relations function, in letting adult participants know that the college is interested in their one-time experience as students. The need for such a canvass is particularly acute in states and localities where adult programs are not self-supporting. With the phenomena of increasing enrollments of this type and dwindling resources for PSE, community colleges will be called upon to account for the benefits—both public and private—which the adult programs and courses produce.

The California Coordinating Council for Higher Education was authorized by the legislature in 1972 to undertake a longitudinal study of community college students, with particular attention to nonpersisters. The legislation was the result of a growing concern about what seemed to be an imbalance between enrollments and degrees and certificates awarded. With enrollments now approaching one million students in nearly one hundred colleges, scarcely more than one hundred thousand students per year can be accounted for as recipients of degrees or certificates or as transfers to baccalaureate institutions. It is no longer possible to refer to the large majority who do not receive such awards and do not transfer as simply participants in continuing education programs. The Coordinating Council study involves more than thirty-two thousand students who registered for credit for the first time in the fall 1972 term in a representative sample of thirty-two colleges. High school students and dropouts, recent high school graduates and others who have delayed college attendance, and transfer students of all ages and levels of educational attainment who have attended other institutions of higher education are included in the survey. (An additional sample of enrollees in noncredit courses will be selected in the fall 1973 term for special study.) The study is directed at persistence and performance in the community colleges, rather than attrition. An operating assumption has been made that students enroll with diverse educational, occupational, and personal objectives which are achieved in programs which may not correspond to catalog and counselor prescriptions, in periods of time which range from less than one term to several years. In other words, no student is described as a dropout until and unless he reports that he is unable to achieve his objectives or the college does not permit him to continue (or to reenroll). This sample will be studied at least through the fall 1975 term.

Few colleges are in a position to undertake all of the types of studies suggested, but they can use the techniques to study areas selected on the basis of priorities assigned to access goals.

V

New Places, Methods, and Modes

Community colleges in many states have gone as far as is fiscally feasible in providing access to PSE on central campuses, using conventional means of instruction. Further expansion of opportunity is not likely to take place on new campuses in sparsely populated areas, to which few students can commute. With little projected growth in enrollments, community colleges are finding it increasingly difficult to add occupational programs which require new, specialized instructional staff and facilities, particularly in areas where enrollments will be small. The ideal of universal access to a comprehensive community college *campus* no longer seems tenable (or even desirable), but the goal of providing universal access to comprehensive postsecondary *education* by means of community colleges is within reach. To attain this goal community colleges must develop both off-campus facilities and new instructional technologies. Some community college programs and services must be taken out into the community, where there are concentrations of people needing such opportunity. At the same time, community colleges must devise new means of relating formal instruction to the diversity of their students' experiences and inject flexibility into the rigid curricular patterns which appear in most college catalogs. The three major areas in which alternatives can be taken are *places, methods,* and *modes* of instruction, new delivery systems for instruction which will take advantage of off-campus locations, new instructional technology, and flexible scheduling.

Both conventional instruction and new technology can be utilized in off-campus programs; on-campus instruction also will benefit from the introduction of new instructional technologies and increased flexibility in programing. Five characteristics of alternative systems are set forth in the Carnegie Commission Report, *The Fourth Revolution* (1972). These characteristics apply to community college planning to expand access: "They [alternative systems] are new, not tradition-bound. They must, by their very nature, develop learning materials that are largely self-instructing. They are, to a considerable extent, mass-oriented, drawing their students from an extremely wide spectrum within American society and, potentially, in very great numbers. This characteristic will enable them to utilize services of individual faculty members in an extremely efficient way. They are physically without boundaries. Their students may be located at considerable distance from the base of operations and from each other. They are not subject to the time restraints imposed by traditional college calendars" (p. 52). The present phenomenon of multicampus community colleges, all attempting to provide comprehensive programs for students able to come to the campuses, may soon give way to a single, relatively small core facility performing certain centralized services and functions, with a virtually unlimited number of educational centers in neighborhoods and other locations where people tend to congregate. Instructional technology makes it possible even now for students in widely dispersed locations to share lectures, demonstrations, discussions, laboratory exercises, resource materials, and evaluation devices.

The education profession has been demonstrably reluctant to take advantage of the new technology for varied reasons. At one extreme is the fear of imposition of a state or national system of education, with standardized curricula supplied to all colleges via television and other electronic means. More realistic, perhaps, is a community college fear of domination by state universities to which their students transfer. On what grounds are they to turn down an offer of videotaped lectures by university professors who are eminent in their fields, for use in transfer courses? More realistic still is the fear of loss of jobs, if the instructor in the classroom is supplanted by an electronic device which is capable of repeating instruction to an unlimited number of students as many times as necessary to achieve a particular level of performance.

A necessary distinction between off-campus instructional alternatives and the new instructional technology may be used in either situation. Similarly, conventional instructional methods may be used both at off-campus and on-campus locations. New approaches to scheduling, flexibility in course sequencing, and variance in enrollment patterns are also applicable to on-campus instruction and are usually a necessity in off-campus instruction. Community colleges which have adopted goals to improve and expand access may wish to consider various alternatives involving instruction both on and off the campus. The community college which makes use of several alternatives becomes a kind of broker, or contractor, for clients seeking opportunity for PSE. The college is then not "all things to all people," since it draws upon the resources of the total community in finding opportunities for students with widely varying backgrounds.

Colleges may also use alternatives in order to exercise some control over the enrollment patterns of students already attending, while continuing to increase access to its programs and services. Suppose a college finds that its enrollment projection exceeds its capacity by 10 percent in two years, although it is not yet providing access for residents of certain sections of its service area. In order to accommodate all who plan to enroll and to expand access at the same time, the college might arrange for instruction in one required and one popular elective freshman course to be offered by open-circuit television, to be viewed at home or at neighborhood centers. Certain centers might be located in areas whose residents have relatively poor access to the campus, so as to provide outreach programs while reducing the instructional level on the campus. The outreach centers might also offer tutoring and counseling services, adult education courses, and community service programs tailored to the needs of residents who would be unlikely to participate in such activities on the main campus.

The need for off-campus sites for community college instruction and services is about equal in metropolitan and sparsely populated areas. In both situations, clusters of residents do not have realistic access to the main campus and are better served at off-campus locations where they enroll for a substantial portion of the program in which they are interested. Some students—particularly adults whose primary commitments are to jobs or homemaking—may never enroll in courses offered on the main campus. Others may use the center programs for orientation to the college, after which they transfer their enrollment to the main campus or enroll at both locations.

Off-campus alternatives range in scope and functions from a minicampus offering both credit and noncredit courses and a full range of student services to a one-time, one-course site selected for the convenience of the students requesting the service. A minicampus is established as a branch or satellite of the college and may have a full-time director and support staff to assist students with registration, counseling, educational and career advisement, and certain types of placement. It may have a small reference library, with easy access to the collection on the main campus. With microfilm and microfiche techniques now available, considerable portions of the college library may be duplicated at neighborhood centers. Students enrolled on the campus may also take advantage of neighborhood centers which offer them a quiet place to study, library resources, typewriters and calculators, tutoring, and other assistance with assignments. Minicampuses may also perform social or recreational functions, by providing a meeting place for special interest groups and assisting others, such as softball teams and musical ensembles, with organizational or recruitment problems. Minicampuses generally do not offer a sufficient range of courses to enable students to complete associate degree requirements without spending some time on the main campus; graduates thus have some exposure to the resources of the main campus and can utilize laboratories and other specialized facilities that are not at the centers. Minicampuses are also distinguished from the parent campus by their predominantly adult, part-time, evening enrollment, a majority of which does not follow prescribed sequences of courses leading to degrees and certificates. Centers are also more likely than the main campus to enroll students of all ages with a need for technical or transfer programs with remediation or refresher work in reading, writing, mathematics, and study skills.

Community colleges use other types of community facilities for less comprehensive programs and services, often on a semipermanent basis. High school facilities are a common locus for night courses, particularly in communities in which the community college has been given full responsibility for adult education. High school facilities are unattractive to potential college students who have had a bad experience as high school students in the facility, however. Centers planned for low-income, urban areas are thus more likely to attract students if they are located in facilities other than high schools. Elsewhere, community colleges have successfully attracted evening students to high schools from which they may have graduated, but the college instructor is disadvantaged in using another teacher's desk, chalkboard, and other facilities. The type of community facilities the college seeks for satellite centers depends upon both the commitment of the college to establish programs and services off the campus and the availability of space at no (or reasonable)' cost.

An alternative to the minicampus and high school centers is a small headquarters office for the neighborhood center, with courses and programs dispersed in many convenient places where people congregate for other purposes. The headquarters site is selected on the basis of high visibility, as well as accessibility to residents during both day and evening hours. Headquarters can serve multiple functions: giving out information about college programs and services, listening to what the community says about its interests and needs for PSE, responding to perceived needs by arranging appropriate courses and programs to be offered in convenient locations, and providing community identification with the parent college by whatever means possible. Some colleges require all students to register at the center headquarters; others permit students to complete necessary registration forms when they enroll for classes at the site, often on the first day of class; this is workable only when registration procedures are very simple and do not require determination of residency status, complex fee structures, and so forth. Courses may be offered in a variety of locations convenient for potential students, often at no cost except for janitorial services for the time the facility is in use. A few available locations are commons or conference rooms in public housing projects, buildings owned by civic and fraternal organizations, churches, libraries, government office buildings, industrial complexes, community centers, and shopping malls. Some locations will be used only once, or infrequently; at others the college will offer courses continuously. Headquarters and scattered program sites have the advantage of developing a community identity with the parent college at considerable less cost than the operation of a minicampus.

Decentralized instruction in locations convenient to residents is an alternative which requires no headquarters. Off-campus programs can be administered from an office on the main campus, with a coordinator responsible for insuring continuity in meeting the needs of the special groups enrolled off the campus. The coordinator may be assisted by teams of support staff who will make periodic visits to the off-campus sites to register and counsel students, explain college programs and policies, and assess the extent to which needs are being met. Or a mobile van can take college personnel and services to the off-campus instructional sites. The van may transport library and other types of instructional materials, art exhibits, miniaturized laboratory demonstrations, and specialized personnel for counseling, testing, career guidance, and other college functions. The van has high visibility for the college as it travels around the community, flexibility in delivering materials and services to multiple instructional sites, and moderate cost, compared with the cost of leasing facilities for a minicampus operation. Mobile vans can also be used by community colleges for recruitment and counseling services in their communities, with no linkage to off-campus instructional sites. The vans have been used primarily in areas with high concentrations of low-income and minority-group residents, in an attempt to increase the proportions enrolling in community colleges. While vans will continue to be used for this purpose, the special federal funding which made their initial operation possible is no longer offered.

Storefronts offering off-campus instruction and services may be found in urban locations which people have largely abandoned, rather than at sites where potential students congregate for other purposes. Storefront operations are low cost and have moderate visibility for a short period of time. Storefront operations have been called "Kleenex colleges," as a way of depicting their disposability after brief use; they have limited usefulness unless remodeled extensively into a flexible instructional facility.

In rural areas, time and distance are barriers to campus access, particularly in areas with long winter months of bad weather. Community colleges serving such areas may establish off-campus centers to which residents may come for some portion of the programs offered by the parent college. In urban areas, access is a more complex phenomenon involving real (cost of books and transportation) and perceived (lack of information about or identity with the college) barriers to attendance. Residents may perceive neighborhood centers as an attempt by the college to keep them away from the campus in sometimes segregated, second-class facilities. In other centers, students may not wish to transfer to the parent campus and request that full programs be offered at the centers and that they be elevated to full campus status. Off-campus programs need to change perceptions and eliminate other barriers to access which keep the urban poor from participating fully in PSE.

Community facilities that are associated with business and industry, government, social services, health care, and recreation would benefit students, faculty, and the college generally. Students benefit by the increased relevance of the setting to student objectives, the chance to explore an occupational field before making a firm commitment to it, classroom instruction combined with practical work experience, and, under some conditions, a chance to earn money and a potential for future placement in full-time employment. Community college faculty benefit from a refresher experience in the field. The college gains by reducing the need for campus facilities, sometimes in fields requiring specialized facilities or expensive equipment.

Federal funding is available for both cooperative education and college work-study programs under the Higher Education Act of 1965 and the 1972 Amendments to the Act. The 1972 Amendments added a provision for a "community service learning program" as part of the work-study activity, which permits students to engage in "projects designed to improve community services or solve particular problems in the community." *Community service* is defined to include work in such fields as environmental quality, health care, education, welfare, public safety, crime prevention and control, transportation, recreation, housing and neighborhood improvement, rural development, conservation, beautification, and "other fields of human betterment and community improvement." Additional federal funding is available to community colleges for cooperative vocational education and work-study programs under the Vocational Education Act of 1963, which is administered as part of an annually updated State Plan for Vocational Education. Community colleges with imaginative staff in planning and development will also find funding for getting students into the many federal programs whose primary mission is not education, such as model cities, labor, conservation, and commerce.

Community colleges have largely ignored private postsecondary schools which offer vocational and technical training, except to avoid offering programs in competition with these schools, especially in the fields of secretarial science and cosmetology. Community colleges have been reluctant to award credit toward associate degrees for occupational courses taken at private schools. But this is changing. Public funds for student financial aid may now be used for enrollment at approved private postsecondary schools offering occupational training, as well as at private collegiate institutions. The Higher Education Amendments of 1972 mandate the inclusion of these schools in statewide planning for PSE as part of the work of commissions which were formerly concerned only with public collegiate institutions. At the same time, a number of states are taking the initiative in making inventories of programs available in proprietary schools and exploring ways of utilizing the resources which such schools could offer to a comprehensive plan for PSE. State advisory councils for vocational education, established under the federal Vocational Education Act of 1963, may assist state PSE agencies in these attempts to involve private PSE. Public funds may even be made available for community colleges (or state commissions) to enter into contracts with proprietary schools for programs not otherwise available to residents of particular areas, consistent with the objectives of comprehensive statewide planning.

PSE can now be made available in homes, factories, offices, and wherever people have television sets (bars!). Cable television can be used to expand the variety and ease of educational experiences which can be made available at low cost to students who might never come to the campus. But, traditional reluctance by both faculty and students to take full advantage of instructional technology is compounded by zero enrollment growth and a surplus of instructors. Technology will in all probability be limited to expanding access and improving instruction for students already enrolling. At stake is the right of the college and its faculty to determine who will teach what to whom, under what circumstances, in programs leading to associate degrees and certificates and for purposes of transfer. Technology is seen as a threat to local autonomy and to the faculty who fear displacement by the electronic medium. Students, however, have the ultimate veto over what the college offers and how it is offered, by virtue of their right not to enroll. Students have shown high interest in nontraditional modes of learning, external degree programs, the awarding of credit for experiences obtained outside the classroom, nonpunative grading, and other options which have not been previously available to students. Thus it is not impossible that students who have been rebelling against poor or impersonal instruction, lack of flexibility in requirements, and irrelevance of the prescribed curriculum may turn to self-directed modes of instruction which have been shunned in the past, including the television medium. Still, many changes have occurred in campus-based instruction which are resulting in higher success rates and improved learning, generally without replacement of the instructor.

Whether or not the new instructional technology is used at the campus, it will surely be used to expand and improve access to PSE for persons unable to come to the campus or unable to benefit from conventional instruction. The Carnegie Commission (1972) provides a succinct, useful summary of what is currently or soon to become available, projections of probable usage through the year 2010, and a few illustrations of exemplary applications of technology, particularly in other nations. The Commission also makes extensive recommendations for expanded state and federal support of developments in instructional technology, including the voluntary organization of regional cooperative learning-technology centers which would share "costs and facilities for the accelerated development and utilization of instructional technology in higher education" (p. 54). The major functions of learning-technology centers would be the identity, production, and distribution of teaching and learning materials appropriate for college instruction; the provision of centralized computing, information services, and large-scale production facilities; and other professional services of the type commonly performed by research and development centers and educational clearinghouses. Federal action is unlikely to implement the most important recommendations of the Commission soon, but community college planners should be aware of certain activities at the federal level which have implication for the expansion of instructional technology in community colleges.

A National Institute for Education, created in the Department of HEW by the 1972 Higher Education Amendments, is assuming certain responsibilities formerly assigned to the National Center for Educational Technology in the U.S. Office of Education. These responsibilities include support for technology demonstration projects pertaining to satellites, open-learning systems, cable television, and other research, planning, and evaluation activities relating to technology (memo from the director of the National Center for Educational Technology, June 3, 1973). A task force on educational technology and productivity is to be established at the Institute to coordinate research and development activities.

Community colleges have attempted to maintain classes which are small enough to attend to individual needs and different learning styles and abilities. This characteristic interest in teaching has distinguished the community colleges from the university, where large classes and the use of inexperienced teaching assistants tend to be dominant at the lower division level. Very rapid increases in enrollments have made it difficult to maintain the low student-instructor ratio. Furthermore, the increased recruitment of students with severe handicaps to learning has heightened the need for individualized instruction in community colleges for the large numbers of underprepared students. One response to this problem increased the amount of time which underprepared students spent in remedial courses and programs, such as two-year "developmental" programs in place of one-year or one-semester programs, and six-hour courses in place of three. Students did not achieve much success, and the problem of providing individualized instruction was solved only temporarily. While small classes were maintained in some courses, lecture-discussion type courses experienced moderate increases in class size, to fifty or sixty students. This solution has also been unsatisfactory; few students can be given special attention in even moderate sized classes.

The twin problems of maintaining small classes and individualizing instruction are being solved by community colleges which develop self-instructional packages, learning laboratories with several media available for individual use, and multimedia classrooms. Learning laboratories and self-instructional packages may be developed by colleges with budgets too low for special equipment. Packages of materials are given to students to master at their own rate, with assistance from the instructor as needed. The most elementary form of these packages includes an instruction sheet for each unit to be mastered, with behavioral objectives for the unit, pretests and posttests of mastery of the objectives, and references to material to be read or examined—textbook assignments, additional reference materials, exhibits, demonstrations, or other learning experiences. More sophisticated packages use tapes, slides, films, specimens, and miniaturized laboratory demonstrations, as well as written materials. With the self-instructional units, the student can work at his own best pace, at a time and place of his own choosing, with options concerning the amount of effort to be devoted to achieving particular objectives. The instructor can work with individual students needing special assistance and can modify packages to include a different amount or type of material. Self-instructional packages may be used in neighborhood centers as well as in campus facilities, with arrangements for student access to instruction during specified hours at the center or by telephone.

Self-instructional units might be compared with correspondence courses insofar as the student takes responsibility for pacing and directing his own learning in both situations. Technology has made it possible to vary the media which are used in campus-based in-

structional packages, thus improving the chances for success of students with different learning styles. Individualized instruction has
been used successfully by community colleges for portions of occupational curricula and in all areas of general education.

Community colleges in Oregon have been noteworthy in
their efforts to develop self-instructional materials as a result of a
statewide Program for the Improvement of Instruction which was
first funded by the Oregon Legislature in 1969, the purpose of which
was "to improve teaching and enhance learning in public two-year
and four-year higher educational institutions" (Northwest Regional
Educational Laboratory, 1973). Projects have been proposed by departments in single institutions in some cases, or by groups of colleges
in others. In the most recent competition for funding, proposals
made by community colleges concerned, for the most part, preparation of self-instructional units in such occupational curricula as
forestry, nursing, and electronics. Thirty exemplary projects were
described in the Regional Laboratory report, among them community college projects involving the use of self-instructional (or
autotutorial approaches) in the areas of mathematics, developmental
writing, communication skills, biology, physical science, and electronics.

Still another exemplary use of self-instructional materials is
demonstrated by Mt. San Jacinto College, a California community
college enrolling only eighteen hundred students in a sparsely populated area. The college achieves individualized instruction by a
combination of multimedia instructional systems, tutorial instruction,
and classes organized as "small group sessions," "general assembly
sessions," and "individual sessions." In addition, terminal behavioral
objectives have been developed for all courses offered by the college,
by instructors employed during the summer. In the words of the
college catalog, "Goals which are clear, complete, and concise in the
minds of both parties do not mislead, become irrelevant, unfair, or
useless." Once objectives are established for particular courses, appropriate materials are placed in the Instructional Center, where
students may check out audiovisual materials for private viewing
and study. A qualified instructor is always available at the center to
assist students.

The learning laboratory offers still another type of self-paced, individualized instruction which permits community colleges to maintain their climate of heightened interest in student learning. The laboratory is by definition a physical facility—not necessarily on the campus—to which students come for some (or all) of their instruction in a variety of courses. Learning laboratories may be specialized, or open to instruction in all areas for which appropriate experiences have been planned. Technology ranges from a simple tape recorder with headphones to a sophisticated dial access system which is connected to a central distribution system for videotapes, recordings, and other audiovisual materials. Microfilm and microfiche libraries may also be included in the holdings of the learning laboratories. On many community college campuses, libraries have been converted into learning laboratories, with individual carrels to which students may check out tapes and slides as well as books. In the future, community college libraries which are primarily book and periodical collections may well be incorporated into learning laboratories, which will be under the direction of a specialist in instructional strategies. (One of the problems facing community colleges is the lack of training opportunities for persons to take charge of learning laboratories; neither librarians nor audiovisual specialists are trained for this function.)

One of the earliest colleges to establish a learning laboratory with sophisticated electronic equipment and campuswide application was Miami-Dade Junior College in Florida. The laboratory is located in the building housing the library, but the planner understood both teaching-learning strategies and the technology required by a multimedia approach to instruction.

Learning laboratories appear to have advantages over conventional classroom instruction in courses designed to build basic communication and computation skills for students with varying levels of preparation for college. Laboratory instruction requires the student to be an active learner, in contrast with the often passive role he assumes in the classroom. He paces himself in the laboratory, often scheduling his own hours. He seeks assistance from the instructor when he needs it but works independently during most of his time in the laboratory. Under optimum conditions each student follows an individually prescribed course of study, based on his initial performance on placement tests. Types and amounts of material may be varied, as well as the level at which the student enters the skill-building course. The course prescription may be modified from time to time as the student achieves more (or less) than expected in relation to the amount of effort he puts forth; a student may even be moved to another type or level of course during the term if his performance shows poor initial placement. Paraprofessional instructors and peer tutors can form the teaching team for the laboratory, headed by a learning specialist. Counselors may be assigned to the learning laboratory on a part-time basis, to work with students whose academic difficulties do not stem wholly from poor prior preparation. Ideally space is provided for one or more counselors adjacent to the laboratory, where students may drop in without appointments.

Learning laboratories may have sophisticated electronic equipment to individualize instruction; they may also be organized with little more than printed materials and work space arranged to facilitate individual instruction. Students may work in individual carrels or at tables, with space arranged for the instructor to confer with an individual student without disturbing the others. Space also needs to be planned to give students access to materials without disturbing other students. One or more small seminar rooms adjacent to laboratories have proved to be useful for small group instruction or group counseling for students participating extensively in laboratory courses. Or a laboratory can offer computer-assisted instruction under conditions of remote access, probably on a time-sharing basis with other colleges or business and industry. Computer utilization is now generally limited to presenting material to the student, evaluating his responses, and directing the sequences of material to be learned, on the basis of the correctness of his responses. Future uses may computerize multimedia presentations of material to students with different needs and abilities and provide group feedback to the instructor so he can improve course content, sequences of learning experiences, and evaluation exercises.

Most community colleges, however, will start by equipping their learning laboratories with less sophisticated devices than computer terminals. Individual carrels will have facilities for listening to tapes; viewing slides, films, and other visuals; and conducting small experiments or witnessing miniaturized demonstrations. In addition, laboratory stations may have dial-access equipment which enables the student to have direct, immediate access to a vast amount of material stored centrally on the campus or at a remote location.

Multimedia classrooms also expand access through improving instruction. Students have diverse learning styles requiring a variety of approaches to instruction, including, but not limited to direct instruction. The lecture-discussion method is less effective for most community college students than for students in four-year institutions. The levels of reading and writing skills of many community college students effectively prevents their participation in lecture courses in which large quantities of reading material are assigned as a basis for discussion or recitation. Past practice has been to place such students in remedial courses in basic communication skills or in vocational programs requiring little reading and writing activity, but the students rejected these programs. The combination of learning laboratories to build basic skills, and multimedia classrooms to vary the mode of instruction in regular college courses appear to offer much more promise for these students.

Multimedia classrooms are generally large instructional areas seating perhaps hundreds of students, which are equipped to allow the instructor (the "director of learning") to use films, slides, videotapes, audiotapes, live demonstrations, and live interviews or lectures from remote locations. Equipment and materials do not have to be transported to the classroom, and live demonstrations can be magnified to enable large numbers of students to witness them simultaneously. Audio amplification is as important as visual magnification in multimedia classrooms; students can then ask questions from widely dispersed seats in forum-type classrooms (or from remote locations on and off campus), and guest lecturers-discussants can be heard by and interact with students by means of telephone connections. Golden West and Orange Coast colleges in California have been in the forefront in constructing multimedia classrooms called *forums,* seating more than three hundred fifty students. Miami-Dade Junior College also has extensive, successful experiences in using multimedia classrooms (auditoriums) to instruct large groups in general education classes.

Instruction in multimedia classrooms must be supplemented by small group discussions, opportunities to ask questions and obtain clarification from instructors, feedback mechanisms to the instructor about the class, and educational and career advisement. Additional arrangements may also be needed for the evaluation of achievement of noncognitive and other objectives which are not readily measured by paper-and-pencil tests.

Access to multiple options available in community colleges may thus be increased by the use of unconventional modes of instruction on the campus, which may be adapted to the differing levels of preparation and learning styles of students entering community colleges. The combined use of learning laboratories for individualized instruction, multimedia classrooms for large group instruction, and self-instructional packages for independent study should enable community colleges to offer enhanced opportunity for the new type of students enrolling in larger numbers each year.

Besides exploring alternatives for campus programs and direct instruction, planners attempting to expand access and improve opportunity must consider college policies and practices which affect access, particularly for nontraditional students. Colleges tend to establish enrollment policies which meet the test of administrative convenience (or tidiness) but fail to increase access. Students are expected to apply for admission (or readmission) by a particular date, obtain advisement and be registered during a prescribed period, add and drop courses by a given date, enroll in a prescribed sequence of courses, and complete courses during a single semester or quarter. The college can then do its academic and fiscal bookkeeping in an efficient, professional manner, but nontraditional students may not know the dates by which applications must be filed and registration completed. Most community colleges impose still additional conditions for enrollment, each with its own due dates—nationally administered tests to be taken (with an associated fee), transcripts to be submitted, and medical history and applications for student aid to be filed (a college permits open admissions until the first day of class but establishes an early cut-off date for receipt of applications for aid). In the past colleges often established policies involving due dates to control the size of enrollments and discourage nontraditional students from enrolling, but now colleges with an explicit policy of open-door admissions subvert the intent of their admissions policy by establishing due dates. Prospective students who are eligible only under a policy of open admissions tend to have other problems or be in circumstances which mediate against their compliance with policies which appear irrational to them.

Colleges which create flexible policies governing admissions and enrollment may adopt still other policies which act as barriers. A few such policy areas are (1) the rigid prescription of courses to be taken by first-time freshmen, including remedial courses by those failing to earn satisfactory scores on placement tests; (2) an advisement system which requires all students to have their programs of of courses approved by an assigned advisor but makes no provision for the in-depth advisement needed by some; (3) the assignment of penalty grades for courses not completed within a specified period of time and an early date by which courses must be dropped; (4) the scheduling of required courses at times inconvenient to students who work off campus; (5) refusal to award credit for relevant work or life experiences and placing restrictions on the acceptance of credit earned at other institutions; (6) the limitation of credit by examination to students who have demonstrated their ability to do college work while attending the college; and (7) readmission procedures which discourage students from returning, and retention policies which make it difficult for readmitted students with past poor records to stay in school.

This list is not exhaustive; it simply illustrates ways in which colleges with open-door admissions policies may adopt other policies which tend to subvert the goals for access which an open admissions program should achieve.

Expanding access also necessitates a variety of flexible arrangements of ongoing programs and services, some involving single colleges and others multiinstitutional. Community colleges have resisted ways to increase flexibility. The building boom in new community college campuses during the past decade resulted in little attention to developing delivery systems in well-established colleges. Second, the concept of comprehensiveness has tended to be equated with self-sufficiency, so individual colleges have attempted to build campuses and facilities to house a full complement of occupational, transfer, general education, and continuing education programs. When particular campuses could not be expanded further, or when student enrollment projections exceeded what was regarded as an optimum size, the solution has been to build a second campus, rather than seek opportunities with other colleges for facilities sharing or concurrent enrollments.

The third inhibiting factor is funding mechanisms by which community colleges in many states receive state or federal support for vocational education. Colleges qualify for support for only the students enrolled in approved courses and programs which start at the beginning of the semester or quarter and continue for the entire term. Until recently, the California community colleges were required to have a credentialed instructor present in the classroom in courses for which state support was received, thus discouraging colleges from adopting new approaches to individualized instruction. Community colleges are unwilling to risk decreased state support by adopting instructional technologies or making cooperative agreements with other colleges. Finally, community colleges have been reluctant to expand their articulation efforts beyond perfecting the smooth flow of students from high school to community colleges to four-year institutions. Less attention has been given to possible sharing of facilities and programs by the different sectors. Concern with protecting the integrity of high school functions has stood in the way of developing cooperative arrangements serving the best interests of students—for example, the admission to college of students without high school diplomas who could profit from a different type of instruction.

If funding problems can be solved, area or regional arrangements involving both groups of community colleges and combinations of community colleges and four-year institutions offer considerable promise of substantially increasing access without expanding community college facilities. Community colleges may exchange students in high-cost programs, thus increasing options for students without duplicating programs at adjacent community colleges. Both (or all) institutions could offer the first year of a specialized program and send students to a single campus offering the second year of the program. This works particularly well for small community colleges whose enrollment does not justify offering a large number of occupational programs requiring special facilities and staff and for programs in which attrition is high at the end of the first year. In metropolitan areas students often find it as convenient to commute to a campus outside the district of residence as to their "local" college, since district boundaries are more often based on political than geographical considerations. The potential loss of state funding can be offset in urban areas if colleges agree upon specialized programs to offer at the second-year level. In sparsely populated areas, community college students may have to move to centers where sufficient numbers of students justify offering second-year courses. Students who are unable to live at home should be given financial aid by the states, in the interest of equalizing access for students in sparsely populated areas.

Regional arrangements may also be made in which community college students are registered on their home campus, for purposes of funding, but attend one or more classes elsewhere. The host institution may simply provide classroom or laboratory space in which the community college conducts classes, using its own staff and course syllabi. Or the host institution can offer nearby community colleges an opportunity to enroll their students in regularly scheduled courses on a space-available basis, at no additional cost and without regard to student eligibility for admission to the host institution. Still another type of cooperation involves sharing specialized equipment such as computers and broadcast television equipment, on either a time-sharing basis, where costs are shared, or at no cost, on a time-available basis.

Title III of the Higher Education Act of 1965, "Strengthening Developing Institutions," has provided incentives to community colleges to establish consortium and other cooperative arrangements for sharing resources both regionally and across state lines, often with assistance provided by four-year institutions in programs to improve instruction and services in the community colleges. Both costs and resources are shared by cooperating institutions, with one college designated as coordinator of administrative functions. Colleges participating in consortia have access to library collections, computers, television courses, instructional materials and equipment, specialized staff, and cooperative research endeavors which they could not individually afford.

Community colleges in isolated areas may also expand access by making their facilities available to four-year institutions offering external degree programs at the baccalaureate level. People residing within commuting distance of a community college are thus enabled to undertake upper division work on a part-time basis without having to move to a location within commuting distance of a senior institution. Shasta College in northern California has cooperated with California State University at Chico in doing this. No course work is required at the Chico campus, but Chico supplies faculty, books, and other instructional materials to supplement community college holdings. The Shasta-Chico program appears to be a prototype for external degree programs offered for part-time, upper division students in California who are unable to pursue degrees on senior college campuses.

Individual colleges may also provide flexible scheduling of courses and programs, so new students need not enter programs at the beginning of regular terms and other students can complete courses in either more or less than a full semester or year. Students without realistic access to PSE are often not available for college entrance at conventional times because of temporary employment or absence from the locality; they need more than the customary amount of time to complete courses with passing grades. Semester-long courses starting on a specified date are a convenience for the college, but may not fit the life styles of nontraditional students. Repeating a course which might be completed in an additional month of study is costly to both student and institution. Flexibility in starting and completing courses is likely to increase completion rates without repetition of courses. The semester or quarter may be subdivided into periods varying from one to six weeks, during which students might take one course (or a limited number) for a relatively short period of time with intensive instruction. Colleges may also schedule breaks between terms so students can enroll for an additional unit of elective credit during the break. A college can conduct a continuous admission-registration program; new students have to wait no more than a few weeks to start classes.

Still another arrangement which appears to be popular with both colleges and part-time students is the so-called weekend college, in which students enroll for Friday night and Saturday, or Saturday and Sunday classes, in programs leading to an associate degree or certificate. In the weekend college these part-time students not only have efficient means to work towards the achievement of their educational objectives, but they also experience camaraderie which is often lacking among evening and other part-time students.

The cluster college arrangement is still another approach for community colleges to consider in attempting to increase access. Specialized interests may be served in cluster colleges; individual needs are more closely tended to than at a single college with an enrollment of five thousand or more students. Few community colleges have developed cluster colleges to date, perhaps because they group students as occupational, transfer, developmental, and adult. These groupings, however, disregard that most students are a kind of "latent occupational"; they may be designated transfer or other when they have simply not yet made an occupational choice. Multi-campus colleges are a kind of cluster of colleges under one administration, but they are less likely to attempt to meet the special needs of particular students than cluster colleges are. Ethnic studies programs, often with related student services, also constitute a kind of cluster college within the community college. Still, larger community colleges seeking ways to personalize instruction and to establish a heightened sense of identity between student and college might well consider the creation of cluster colleges based on models provided by four-year institutions.

Three examples of noteworthy alternatives to conventional ways of offering instruction have been selected for presentation because of the extent of their departure from tradition. The first is the Television College unit of the multicampus Chicago city colleges. The Television College has been offering college-level instruction for credit by open-circuit television for more than ten years. Instruction is offered in about nine courses each term, for twenty-five hours of broadcasting per week. Students have earned associate degrees without enrolling for campus-based instruction. More have persisted for years without seeking degrees, and countless thousands view courses without registering for credit. The college serves the chronically ill and handicapped, prisoners, and others unable to come to the campus for instruction. Offering television courses for credit is commonplace, but the Television College is unique in delivering an associate degree program to off-campus students.

The second example is the Urban Centers established by the State University of New York in 1966, in cooperation with selected community colleges. The centers were created as a statewide effort to deliver PSE to the urban disadvantaged who were ineligible for admission and otherwise lacked access to community colleges. Local community colleges were either unable to meet these needs because of other priorities or unwilling because of the lack of readiness of potential students for regular college work. Programs at the centers include short-term, noncredit vocational programs not available at the colleges, college readiness courses for students preparing to enter degree programs on the campuses, basic education necessary for success in vocational programs and on the job, and student services, including job development and placement. The centers are located away from the parent campuses, in areas accessible to the urban poor and minorities.

Finally, the Northern California Area Planning Council for Educational Programs, comprised of six community colleges and two public four-year institutions, has focused on regional planning to meet manpower needs, new and better educational delivery systems to serve residents of sparsely populated areas, and new programs of continuing education for out-of-school adults. The colleges have undertaken cooperative research, planning, and development of programs in a way which other colleges in sparsely populated areas might well emulate.

VI

Program Goals

$\mathbf{D}$efining program goals in community colleges is no less important than setting goals for access, since access to institutions is of limited social value unless people are interested and can succeed in the available programs. Program goals reflect philosophies about the relationship of the individual to society and the importance of the individual interests in relation to manpower needs. Probably the most important characteristic which distinguishes the community college from the technical institute is its paramount concern with individual needs and interests. Community colleges are interested in educating whole persons, not simply the labor-force portion of the person.

Views on failure constitute still another philosophic consideration in setting program goals. To what extent should students be permitted to enroll in programs in which they are likely to fail? How many times should they be allowed to repeat programs in which they have failed (or try new programs)? Of what value is failure as a learning experience?

112

Community colleges are committed to offering general education, occupational education, two-year curricula parallel to those offered by baccalaureate institutions, and some type of continuing education for part-time students. In addition, most colleges develop student services, which include counseling at a minimum, and now also acknowledge their obligation to provide special programs and services for students who are underprepared for regular college programs. Community college governing boards choose among several different ways of conducting these programs, but their choice depends on the framework of broad program goals, within which specific options may be evaluated.

The most important (and probably the most difficult) broad program goal is the desired distribution or balance of students among the major categories of programs. Is the two-to-one ratio of students in transfer versus occupational programs an acceptable balance? What proportion of students will be tolerated in remedial or developmental programs? How large may continuing education become before causing undesirable imbalances in the overall distribution of students among major programs? A goal stating the desirable distribution of students among programs is not incompatible with the open-admissions philosophy if the PSE needs of the community are clearly understood by the goal-setters. An explicit goal on the desired balance among programs provides a basis for decisions about the allocation (or reallocation) of resources. Numbers of curricula or course offerings in the major program categories do not give the number of students per program, and a preliminary broad goal must relate proportions of students to categories of programs.

The second broad category of goals relates student interests to manpower needs. To what extent should the college try to meet local, regional, or statewide needs for certain categories of trained manpower? Should occupational curricula be developed in anticipation of new or increasing needs? Planners should first state how they want the community college to respond to the need for trained manpower. Then they should state how they want the college to respond to students who express interest in specialized training for less needed jobs. Third, planners should state college goals for career education, including career counseling for transfer students and cooperative education or work experience. Finally, a goal should be established with respect to job placement, perhaps specifying the desired relationship between job preparation received at the college and consequent employment. For example, is the college satisfied if half its graduates from occupational programs work in jobs unrelated to their preparation? Consideration of these goals will lead planners to additional goals in the category of student interests versus societal needs.

Goals are also needed in the area of transfer and articulation; these should reflect student aspirations and achievements as well as transfer agreements. The colleges appear to have student-related goals now that cover more than transfer programs in the community college and upper division programs in baccalaureate institutions. Since student performance after transfer has been generally satisfactory, community colleges have become somewhat complacent. A goal should be stated which establishes an acceptable ratio of transfer students to those who actually transfer to four-year institutions during a given period of time. Another goal should state the desired grade-point differential between the community college and four-year institutions, specifically plus, minus, or zero, and the size of the differential, if not zero. While a plus or zero differential might appear to be obviously desirable, the adoption of such a goal implies a common standard for all institutions and programs, without taking into account differences between abilities of students in two-year and four-year colleges. Nonpunative grading policies, under which no grades of D or F are assigned, complicates the goal-setting process still further. Finally planners need to state a commitment with respect to the acceptance of courses and credits earned at the community college. Specifically, how much loss can be tolerated, and under what conditions? Colleges with particular problems, such as large numbers of financially needy students in transfer programs, may have other goals in this area.

College goals for developmental or remedial programs are particularly important because this area often shows uneven success or the lack of measurable goals. A goal cannot state simply a commitment to the improvement of access for disadvantaged and other underprepared students. Rates of desired (and attainable) success have to be explicitly detailed, both for the developmental program and in subsequent programs in which the student may enroll. Rates include placement in college programs and jobs, as well as success in occupational and transfer programs. For example, has the college made a commitment to find an appropriate placement for all students completing developmental programs and wanting to be placed, or will it be satisfied by placement of two-thirds of the students? Will it be satisfied if half the formerly successful developmental students who enroll in transfer programs earn grades of C or better? Again, goals need to be both feasible and desirable; they need to be modified from time to time to either raise expectations or reflect reality based on experience. Time needed to complete developmental programs may be still another goal. Should students be permitted to pace their own instruction? Should flexible scheduling be applied to developmental programs?

Finally, goals need to be established for the delivery of student personnel services—admissions, counseling, testing, co-curricular activities, student government, placement, and health. Goals should constitute the college point of view about explicit outcomes or payoffs desired from the organization, administration, and desired staffing patterns of student personnel services. Other goals might reflect desired changes in the attitudes of students and faculty toward the delivery of personnel services. Quantifiable goals statements are more difficult to construct for student personnel services than for instructional programs, but without them, decisions cannot be made about the allocation of resources to this program area.

College catalogs are vivid examples of the apparent indifference academic planners show to the actual student body. Imagine trying to construct a profile of a community college student body merely from an examination of a typical catalog. The catalog devotes substantial space to the four-semester sequence of courses leading to the associate degree in perhaps fifty occupational areas and to the lower division requirements of the four-year institutions to which students are most likely to transfer, together with suggested four-semester programs in selected transfer majors. Brief descriptions follow of all credit courses offered by the college. Neither the table of contents nor the index to the catalog mention remedial or developmental programs. Students who fail to meet certain standards at the time of admission may be shocked to discover these programs for the first time. Potential students who are gifted with perservance may uncover, upon close examination, listings of remedial courses in communication and computational skills. References to adult, evening, and continuing education students are explicit but limited to a paragraph or a page, at most.

Suppose a person knows nothing about the college and wishes to get a total picture from the catalog. He would no doubt imagine a young student body enrolled full-time in freshman and sophomore programs leading either to degrees and certificates in a wide variety of occupational fields or to transfer with the associate degree to a four-year institution. He would note programs for adult and continuing education, community services, and developmental education, but he would have trouble with the points at which these spill over into the area for associate degree programs. He will probably judge by the small amount of space allotted to their description that they have relatively minor significance compared with degree and certificate programs.

If he is interested in admissions, what he will find depends on the catalog. One catalog selected as representative of medium-sized, semiurban colleges states simply, "Any graduate of an accredited high school may be admitted," although this college must accept all high school graduates. The college then notes correctly its discretionary power in admitting high school dropouts of at least eighteen years of age, "when the evidence indicates that the individual will benefit from college level instruction." Both statements apply only to day students, and no conditions are stated about the admission of evening students. Other colleges operating under similar statutes and with open-door policies present rather elaborate statements of philosophy concerning admissions, some stressing the goal of free access for all who seek PSE, others discouraging applicants without conventional preparation while lacking authority to deny them admission.

While community college catalogs are often a poor reflection of the actual student body, they give a fairly true account of the results of academic planning by college officials with respect to curricula leading to degrees and certificates, course offerings, and educational policies. But in reality the community colleges are attracting increasing numbers of part-time, adult students with bonafide educational objectives which are not satisfied in prescribed curricula. The availability of financial aid to students who enroll only part-time may also increase enrollment trends toward larger numbers of part-time students.

A college which continues to plan its future operations on the assumption that a majority of its students will enroll full-time in prescribed curricula, in continuous attendance until graduation, may be doing a poor job of setting goals and allocating resources. A sounder, if less efficient, set of assumptions for projecting academic planning into the future are (1) Most people could profit from some type of PSE at various times in their lives, but full-time college attendance directly after high school is not the best pattern for most; (2) Few people commencing full-time higher education after high school will continue in uninterrupted attendance to the highest level they first expected to achieve; most will stop out periodically, many permanently, from full-time education; (3) Most people will be in the labor force for some significant portion of their adult lives; many will enter it sooner than their original plans for PSE indicate; (4) Few people have no needs which community colleges can meet in programs of continuing education; as people move into and through their chosen careers, they develop new and changing needs for education to improve their functioning in their multiple adult roles.

When planners recognize these general assumptions, they can proceed to make more sound plans for specific programs, such as general education. General education has two distinct connotations in community colleges, both of which have important implications for goal setters. One meaning encompasses the portion of the curriculum which provides breadth in the arts and sciences for students in both occupational and transfer programs. Courses in natural sciences, social sciences, and humanities, and possibly also in communications and mathematics may be considered part of the general education program. Goal setters have to establish an optimum general education requirement for certificate and degree programs in occupational fields, as well as counseling students about the value of general education in relation to their more immediate occupational objectives if they do not intend to complete requirements for a degree.

The other meaning of general education is applied to the educational objectives of students who plan neither to transfer into a baccalaureate program nor to pursue an occupational curriculum. Their program resembles a transfer curriculum but differs in that they may enroll in courses at a different or lower level than required by transfer institutions, and they may select entry-level courses in occupational fields as electives, for which transfer credit might not be awarded by baccalaureate institutions.

This second meaning of general education has special implications for goals in academic planning. First, it dispels a common assumption that students who do not pursue baccalaureate degrees need occupational education. General education students need neither of these. Little is known about the employability of such graduates or about their interest in continuing education. The question is whether the college should ensure all degree candidates either career education or transfer plans or both. Secondly, developmental or remedial programs could become curricula leading to an associate degree in general education. Some community colleges have established full-year developmental curricula, including specially tailored general education courses for students who lack the requisite basic skills to pursue conventional courses. If these students plan to transfer into baccalaureate programs, they are required to repeat their first year, taking courses for which transfer credit is awarded. But colleges now face the question of awarding associate degree credit for developmental courses, so the student can pursue an occupational or other type of major in the second year without repeating basic courses. Is a single, common standard desirable for all students awarded the associate degree, should programs be tailored to the widely differing abilities of students? Efforts have been made over the years to avoid second-class status for students in occupational degree programs. Goal setters might offer similar protection to students with only general education objectives.

Transfer programs, while one of the most successful programs, should also be examined in light of students' actual needs. Considerable community college staff time is devoted each year to maintaining good articulation with baccalaureate institutions to which the largest numbers of their students transfer. Articulation agreements insure the acceptance of courses and credits gained by students completing community college programs. Lower division programs in important transfer majors are reviewed to insure that community college programs are indeed parallel to the programs offered by the transfer institutions. The results of the program reviews and articulation agreements appear as recommendations in community college catalogs. Students can then select both major and transfer institutions when they enter a community college, and if they follow the prescribed program for the particular institution, they are assured of full credit and no time loss in making up requirements when they transfer. But less than a majority of students enrolled in community college transfer programs eventually enroll in baccalaureate programs.

While the success of transfer education is borne out by the performance of students at the upper division level, very little is known about why so many transfer students do not eventually transfer. Were they falsely identified as transfer program students when they entered community college? Are they eligible scholastically to transfer to the institution of their choice? To what extent is lack of financial aid a barrier to transfer? Did students modify their intent to transfer while enrolled at the community college and, if so, should they have been given career counseling at that point? Will they return to the community college for occupational training?

Another aspect of the problem is presented by students in occupational programs whose degree aspirations extend to the baccalaureate degree and beyond. Their lower division programs often include occupational courses taught in somewhat different form at the upper division level in baccalaureate programs, as in the field of nursing, or not at all in senior institutions, as in cosmetology. Efforts to date have been devoted to forcing a kind of articulation where no natural solution exists. The community college has demanded that the baccalaureate institution award elective credit for occupational courses it does not offer itself and that graduates of occupational programs receive full credit for lower division courses toward a bachelor's degree in the same field. Planners have tended to overlook solutions which would either create new types of add-on programs in the bacclaureate institutions (as in the scientific technologies) or make arrangements for students to earn degrees in related fields (sociology for associate degree nurses, personnel psychology for certain business majors with associate degrees, and so forth). Opportunity for access must be opened for community college students with widely varying career interests, while planners realize too how few are likely to transfer immediately after completing community college programs.

Not to offer transfer programs which have been carefully articulated with those in four-year institutions is not a viable community college option. But the dominance of the transfer function tends to limit other community college options, for example, experimentation with new arrangements of courses and delivery systems, in the fear that transfer credit might be denied. Furthermore, student options are limited as an indirect result of this dominance, by effectively denying transfer students opportunities for career counseling and occupational education at the lower division level.

Career education is a program that most young people need, since nearly all will be in the labor force for a significant portion of their lives. Career education includes but is not limited to occupational training. Adolescence is probably the most important time for good career education but it should extend throughout the lives of most workers. In the community college, career education is knowledge about the world of work, skills for use in suitable employment, positive attitudes toward work, and the means to obtain continuing education and guidance throughout the life of the individual worker. As individuals make decisions about employment, they should have access to information, guidance, and training to enable them to move ahead in their careers. The goals of career education are extremely ambitious, since they apply to all students, at widely varying levels of job preparation.

In the past and to a considerable extent still now, community colleges attempt to make a clear distinction between occupational education and other academic programs. Occupational education is developed to prepare students for immediate employment and is thus characterized as *terminal*. The distinction has been generated by federal funding regulations providing for reimbursement of excess costs of occupational programs, and also by articulation agreements with four-year institutions which guarantee the acceptance of credit earned in nonoccupational courses and programs. Opportunities for career education have thus been limited for community college students who are not preparing for specific career fields at the associate or higher degree level.

All young people need career education, perhaps especially students in general education and transfer programs, who may be unable to make a career decision. Also, many students intend to transfer into baccalaureate degree programs which provide occupational preparation, but they leave college before that and enter the labor force without specialized training and often without career counseling. They also generally lack supervised work experience that students in occupational programs have. They may need continuing education after leaving the community college, for upgrading, retraining, or refresher objectives, or they may want to transfer to four-year institutions to pursue baccalaureate degrees. They too need career guidance as they change their levels of aspirations and career interests.

Although the U.S. Bureau of Labor Statistics shows that 80 percent of the jobs in the 1970s require no more than a high school education and secondary schools try to insure that every high school graduate will have marketable job skills, community colleges still need to provide career education. Community colleges may need to concentrate on general education, continuing occupational education, cooperative education, supervised work experience, or transfer programs leading to the professions; community college career education is still necessary to supply trained manpower in areas of manpower shortages. Community colleges should help all students get ready to enter the world of work by ensuring the best possible match of students and jobs in their initial job placements, using characteristics other than specific level of job preparation. This requires a different kind of planning for occupational education than is now common, with more emphasis on the acquisition of basic communication and computational skills, career guidance, and supervised work experience. The following problems and issues point to the potential role of the community colleges in career education.

1. *Scope of occupational education:* Although some young people need job training below the technical and semiprofessional levels, some people feel that community colleges should not train blue-collar workers, apprentices, or people in poverty seeking federally supported manpower training.

2. *Response to community need:* The manpower needs of the local community and of society generally must be weighed against

the interests of students in particular types of career education. Furthermore, the specific needs of local business and industry must be evaluated to determine whether the public is being asked to subsidize training which industry itself should provide.

3. *Access to programs:* Rather than attempting to offer all occupational programs on all campuses, planners should be more concerned with providing access to programs for students from low-income families who may lack transportation to campuses participating in cooperative regional programs of occupational education. The costs of specialized facilities and equipment must be weighed against the need for access to programs on two or more campuses in a district or region.

4. *Meeting nonlocal needs:* The question of preparing local youth for jobs which they will find only outside the college area is most pressing in communities with high local unemployment, declining population, and poor economic conditions. If few local opportunities for employment exist, job markets should be identified in other parts of the state or regions. Sending students away from home to obtain occupational training at community colleges in metropolitan areas with better employment possibilities has been hampered by the organization of colleges into districts which provide considerable support from local taxes for the education of local residents. This problem may be solved, however, as new incentives are made available for cooperative arrangements and new financial aid becomes available to students to use at the institutions of their choice. In addition, retraining may be needed for local experienced workers who suffer from technological unemployment or the relocation of large industries in distant states or regions. Individual needs and preferences need to be reconciled with local and area manpower needs and opportunities. College decisions must also consider developing specialized programs to train a limited number of persons for statewide employment. If, for example, projections show a statewide need for approximately forty new workers prepared in associate degree programs each year for the next ten years, to replace retiring workers, state and local college planning must assure not only that the needs are met but also that colleges do not duplicate their efforts to meet them.

5. *Manpower projections for planning:* Ideally, community colleges should be able to develop occupational programs in time to anticipate both future shortages of trained manpower and new types of jobs requiring specialized training. In reality, community colleges are probably best able to respond to immediate needs for manpower to fill vacancies in established jobs, because of the primacy of student interests, the perceived needs of local employers, and the opportunity for employment after program completion. Student and employer interests in specific programs thus converge on this common ground of employment potential. But the community college, while being responsive to immediate student interests and employer needs in planning occupational education, should not exclude anticipation of future needs based on manpower projections.

6. *Articulation with high schools:* High schools now attempt to equip their graduates for immediate employment, regardless of their educational and career aspirations, and community colleges sometimes ignore these occupational competencies. Community college planners disagree about which programs are appropriate for students who have attained entry job level competencies in high school. Can they profit from additional occupational education before entering full-time employment? Should they be encouraged to seek employment while pursuing some type of continuing education program? Or should they be encouraged to postpone college attendance until they really need PSE? A growing number of occupational programs offered by community colleges are also offered at the secondary school level, but few efforts are made to articulate programs and to make specific provisions for students to transfer from high school to college career education.

Of the several subpopulations enrolled in occupational programs, Caucasian women who are recent high school graduates appear to be best served, especially in nursing and other allied health professions. Large numbers of young women also succeed in secretarial and other business programs. Increasing numbers are enrolling in public service programs to prepare for paraprofessional work in social welfare, education, and library science. Minority group women, particularly black women with only slight educational handicaps, have succeeded in the same occupational programs as

Caucasian women. Others with more severe educational handicaps are progressing more slowly toward career goals but are at least cognizant of goals within their eventual reach.

The same level of success cannot be reported with young male students in occupational education, particularly with minority students. Some of them may be unwilling to commit themselves to terminal education, or they may lack an interest in a particular career field or preparation for technical education. Minority men who graduate from high school with poor preparation for college are particularly fearful of being placed in occupational programs leading to low-status, blue-collar jobs; most of them have insisted upon transfer programs with options leading to professional training. Community college planners may need to reevaluate their programs of occupational training, considering a different type of preparation for large numbers of males under twenty-one years of age. Community college functions in occupational education may be better defined as those of career guidance, supervised work experience, improvement of basic communication and computational skills, and counseling to help individuals to gain insights into their own abilities, needs, and interests, in preparation for entry into the labor force as full-time, adult workers. The community college product has advantages over both the baccalaureate degree holder and the recent high school graduate in entering the labor force. He commands less salary than the entry level workers with four years of PSE who may possess no additional job skills and is more mature than the recent high school graduate who may have the same job skills. The community college does have success, however, with males in their middle twenties and older who are seeking upgrading and changes in occupation after experience. The available career education is appropriate to their needs for careers in business and industry, government, law enforcement and corrections, and in allied health fields. Future occupational education in the community colleges is thus likely to be more closely allied with adult and continuing education functions than with entry-level job preparation for recent high school graduates.

Adult and continuing education is offered at times, in places, and under conditions convenient to adult part-time students. Programs may feature the same credit courses and even the same instructors as regular day programs or they may concentrate on courses uniquely suited to adult needs and interests which do not yield credit for a degree. Public schools in some communities may offer the same programs, since they are not necessarily characterized as collegiate-level courses. The third type of adult education is defined as community service activities, including short-term instructional programs, concerts, forums, lecture series, recreational programs, and human development programs.

Community colleges show a trend to increasing enrollments of part-time students in continuing education programs tailored to the individual's objectives. The students are adults (beyond high school age) who devote less time to education than to other activities such as jobs or homemaking. Several special arrangements are made. In one case, the students may enroll for a limited number of units (usually six) at one time, or for no more than a specified cumulative number of units, without completing full admission procedures (submission of transcripts, placement tests, and health examination, and a detailed admission application). In some instances, students may enroll on the first day of class, without prior application. In another case, students may enroll in courses on either a credit or a no-credit basis, depending upon their individual needs. Some colleges permit students to make decisions about credit as late as the time of the final examination. Or prerequisites for courses may be waived for students who believe that they can profit these courses. Colleges may charge tuition and fees which are not charged for day and full-time students. Charges range from a nominal fee of a few dollars to tuition sufficient to cover the cost of instruction. The courses are offered during late afternoons and evening hours, with regular day students allowed to enroll when they find it more convenient to attend a night class or when day classes in a particular course are overenrolled. Planning for these programs is based on expected demand by evening students, with little attention to sequencing for complete curricula.

Large portions of the course offerings and enrollments are in courses related to occupational objectives. Courses may provide job training or other skills to enhance employment opportunities (such as speech, personnel psychology, or business correspondence), or they may provide entry level preparation, for example, for women entering the labor force for the first time. Other job-related courses may be designed to retrain local workers, sometimes in anticipation of layoffs in the area, or to upgrade individuals eligible for promotion, or to refresh knowledge in technical fields. Federally and state-supported manpower training for entry level jobs, such as that under the Manpower Development Training Act, is usually organized as a noncredit program under the community service or adult education function. Students with occupational objectives may enroll for a single course in which they expect to achieve their limited objectives, or they may pursue a series of courses over several semesters, sometimes on a noncontinuous basis, until an occupational objective is attained. Some part-time adult students work toward (and achieve) associate degrees, both in occupational fields (such as in police science and as social welfare technicians) and in liberal arts fields with no direct employment relationship.

Besides occupation-related courses, adults can take courses in roles such as those of consumer, conservationist, parent, householder, citizen, volunteer social service worker, hobbyist, and retired worker. Reductions in the demand for manpower are creating new leisure time for some adults who normally hold two jobs or work overtime in one. Persons unaccustomed to leisure time are more in need of continuing education than those with active avocational interests which have always occupied their free time. Regular community college course offerings are sufficiently broad that they encompass courses related to most adult roles and functions, including avocational activities. Flexibility with respect to time, place, credit, and conditions for enrollment makes it possible for community colleges to offer adults opportunities for part-time education which include multiple options.

Furthermore, "regular" students are beginning to resemble adult students by choosing nontraditional objectives and attendance patterns and assuming responsible adult roles. The future community college may not distinguish between "day regular" and "adult continuing" education. Instead, the entire college program may be organized as an adult education function, with all the flexibility and options now available to part-time adult students. Supporting student services will take on increased importance, since there will be fewer requirements, prescriptions, and barriers to participation. Degrees and formal transfer arrangements will diminish in importance, since individuals will be encouraged and assisted to formulate idiosyncratic objectives which they can and want to attain.

Noncredit adult education programs may include many of the same types of offerings as are found in the continuing education program for part-time students. Conversational French, tailoring, personnal typing, automobile repair, and landscape gardening all have counterparts in the regular curriculum and in evening programs for part-time students. They enjoy the additional flexibility which is possible in courses in which no students are registered for degree credit; all are enrolled to attain certain personal objectives independent of degree requiremnts. The program has the additional advantage of being able to use specially talented instructors who might be unavailable or unqualified for a regular faculty appointment. Scheduling may also be flexible, and groups of students may request a rescheduling of a special interest class beyond one term if they wish to continue learning together. Under some conditions, groups of potential enrollees may petition for the scheduling of a class not previously offered by the college, if demand is sufficiently high and if the course is not tailored to the unique needs of a particular company or business.

Many adult, noncredit classes do not have counterparts in the regular curriculum. One group is subcollegiate in nature and includes basic adult education for literacy, elementary school subjects, high school subjects leading to an equivalency diploma, and some vocational subjects. Others are special-purpose courses which would not normally be creditable toward an associate degree, although taught at a level which may assume the equivalency of high school graduation. Examples of these are power boat handling, practical legal problems, group leadership training, Americanization, and "creative divorce."

In still other instances, noncredit classes may serve as a vehicle for trying out new types of programs in areas in which the college does not yet offer regular instruction. Particularly in occupational fields in which the college is considering the development of new programs, these classes give planners a chance to learn about community interest and to experiment with content and levels of instruction. The most appropriate occupations for this type of instruction are those which normally employ adults with some prior job experience.

Community service programs allow the greatest amount of flexibility in all types of adult programs, since they need not have instruction as their major function nor be limited to enrolled students. In small communities and sparsely populated areas, the college serves as a major cultural-recreational center. Use of college facilities constitutes only one aspect of a comprehensive community service program, however. The college with an aggressive program will develop *social outreach,* to involve the disadvantaged in college programs; *individual development,* such as women's counseling and career development centers; to provide a resource for data collection relating to community needs and interests; *civic action,* such as neighborhood cleanup campaigns and bond issues; and *conference planning,* to assist community groups in planning workshops, institutes, and conferences (Raines and Myran, 1970).

The most promising way to organize adult and continuing education programs groups all courses offered on an optional credit basis in one unit and all noncredit courses, programs, and experiences in a second, community services unit. In time the "regular" community college program may be absorbed into these two units, as fewer students enroll with firm degree and transfer objectives, in full-time programs and in continuous attendance to the attainment of objectives.

VII

Practice and Purpose

$\mathbf{B}$eginning with a set of important fundamental planning themes, the preceding chapters show how community colleges can be effectively planned and developed during the coming decades. The nature of planning, the behavior of policymakers, and difficulties in currently popular analytical techniques suggest an alternative approach based upon explicit specifications of college goals and objectives. Access is emphasized, bringing together the diverse components of academic facilities and fiscal planning to result in nontraditional methods, programs, and delivery systems.

Now suppose the staff has completed the policy analysis of five planning alternatives. The rankings in Table 10 are reported to policymakers. Alternatives D and E are discarded early because of their general weakness under all three criteria. If alternative A had satisfied the equity criterion, it would have been a clear choice. Alternative B, the next preferred alternative according to benefits and costs, satisfies the equity criterion, but the decrease in economic

Table 10.

RANKINGS OF FIVE PLANNING ALTERNATIVES

Alternative	Benefit Ranking	Costs (Ratio to lowest cost alternative)	Satisfy Equity Criterion	Equity Ranking
A	1	1.00	no	4
B	2	1.30	yes	2
C	4	1.35	yes	1
D	3	1.39	no	5
E	5	1.40	yes	3

efficiency should cause both analysts and decisionmakers to see if A can be modified to satisfy the equity criterion. If the resulting cost of modified A is less than 1.30 and the estimated benefits ranking not disturbed, then the modified A might be the preferable choice. Or is the equity criterion worth the decrease in economic efficiency implied in choosing B, rather than A? Alternative C might then be considered, in view of its "showing" in the equity criterion.

This consideration too requires a subjective trade-off between the three criteria, based upon the judgment of the decisionmaker. No planning model can completely remove the ambiguity that is present when equity, as well as efficiency, considerations are thought to be relevant. Considerable subjective judgment on the part of policy makers is still required, particularly since each of the three rankings represent different measurement units.

If the college educational process is a worthwhile investment, benefits exceed costs and, therefore, benefits should be weighted more heavily than costs. With this in mind, academic (benefit) and fiscal (cost) planning decisions can be made simultaneously and access to community college education is made an explicit part of the planning process. The approach would be used primarily for important decisions regarding college goals and programs, particularly when specific policy objectives remain to be selected.

Suppose a community college contemplates a new program for the elderly residing in its community service area. No such programs exist currently, but college staff and local planning authorities estimate that citizens aged sixty-five and over will increase from 10 to 30 percent of the local population.

Staff complete a survey of the educational needs and preferences of the elderly in the area and find considerable interest in community college programs, primarily in the area of hobbies, recreation, personal development, and certain avocations. Specific courses in preparing income tax returns, on health for the aged, on consumer concerns, and on retirement benefits for the aged are frequently requested. Courses with an option of taking credit are preferred but little apparent interest in degree programs exhibited. Activities with small groups and high participation are preferred. The vast majority of the elderly are scattered throughout the urban area, but mobile home parks, condominium developments, convalescent homes and hospitals, and other types of senior citizen developments are becoming increasingly popular, and most of the increased elderly population growth is likely to reside in them.

Staff has developed the following four alternatives: (A) a program of instructional courses offered totally at night in otherwise unused classrooms on campus located at the edge of the urban area—courses are taken from a variety of disciplines, including some existing courses and two dozen new courses specifically designed for the aged, and limited counseling services are provided; (B) a less extensive program of courses, covering mostly hobbies and recreational activities, all conducted in community facilities at about three dozen locations, including the major elderly centers; (C) a program offering a few multidiscipline instructional courses on campus during the day along with courses in two dozen community facilities; (D) a program similar to C but with considerably more avocational offerings on campus (like A), off-campus offerings (similar again to C), and an extensive recreation and community service program conducted at the various centers for the elderly.

To analyze benefits, staff and community representatives formulated two dozen specific major objectives from the following program goals: (1) learning new hobbies, avocations, and recreational pursuits, (2) learning new or missed educational skills, (3) interacting with the younger generation, (4) deriving satisfaction from the joy of learning, (5) combating loneliness and alienation, and (6) feeling useful and relevant. For the access criterion staff identified nine major subgroups of the elderly: three groups living in major retirement developments; two in mobile home units; and four distributed throughout the urban area categorized into relatively homogeneous subgroups according to housing, transportation problems, and general socioeconomics, all of which correlated highly in each case. Multi-year costs are also estimated for each of the four alternatives, and Table 11 shows the resulting sets

Table 11.
RANKINGS FOR ELDERLY PROGRAM ALTERNATIVES

Alternatives	Benefits (objectives satisfied of the 24 specified)	Costs (ratio of least cost alternative)	Access (equity) ranking
A	19	1.00	4
B	16	1.20	2
C	13	1.25	3
D	21	1.60	1

of rankings. Alternative A costs the least because classes are conducted at virtually no facilities expense. Yet it is least accessible, with night programs, transportation needed, and total lack of community coverage. Alternative B is not overly expensive, provides reasonably good access with locations throughout the community, but would not satisfy about one-third of the desired objectives, particularly those dealing with intergenerational activity and the learning of new educational skills. Alternative C is less desirable than B on all three counts.

The most desirable alternative in terms of benefits and access is, as one might expect, the most costly. Faced with this dilemma, policymakers have staff develop a fifth program alternative by modifying D to reduce the number of daytime courses, combining several with resulting anticipated larger class sizes; add several night courses at the elderly centers; and use primarily elderly volunteers as faculty off campus and reclassify such courses to be noncredit or for credit at the option of those attending. These measures reduce the cost of alternative D to 30 percent more than that of A, or 1.30, and benefits or outcomes are increased by the greater participation of elderly as faculty as well as students. Policymakers feel the cost is now feasible and select D, as modified, demonstrating their high evaluation of access to programs and program outcomes. While the final decisions are subjective, the process does have the beneficial impact of clearly identifying the issues and consequent analyses of cost-program trade-offs and the two dozen specified objectives which provide the basis for evaluation of actual program results and possible reformulation and improvement during a future planning round.

Consider a broader planning problem, involving the general operating mode of a community college district during the next three decades. The district currently has five thousand students enrolled at one college located in the major urban center of the district and is situated so that unlimited expansion is possible. Long-term enrollment projections indicate a total enrollment of ten thousand in fifteen years, after which growth will be minimal. Staff has identified the following as feasible policy alternatives: (A) expand the existing campus to ultimately handle the total ten thousand students; (B) add one new campus to handle the additional five thousand students; (C) add two new centers, each to handle about half the additional students; (D) add two new comprehensive campuses, and distribute all students equally among the three; and (E) accommodate all ten thousand on the existing campus and gradually increase the number of small neighborhood satellite centers, so that fifty or sixty are established after the first decade.

Estimates of projected costs include both facility and operating public costs as well as transportation and other private costs facing students and their families for each policy alternative. Benefits rankings for each alternative are constructed by an extensive examination of resulting institutional and student characteristics according to five major categories of outcomes: (1) whole-person value added, (2) specialized-person value added, and the transitory benefits of (3) immediate experience, (4) individual need fulfillment, and (5) immediate community benefit.

The analysis may begin with peer-group contact, which is estimated to have direct and primary impact upon whole-person value added but only secondary impact upon specialized-person value added. Further, peer group contact is important for the student's immediate experience both intellectually and socially and provides the opportunity for the fulfillment of social needs. College staff analyzes each of the five policy alternatives to determine the extent to which each provides the opportunity for informal peer-group contact among students outside class. In general, the larger campus tends to reduce such contacts, though the functional organization of units on even the large campus may be sufficiently small to encourage such interaction. Staff analysis continues similarly through two dozen remaining institutional and student characteristics. In each case the relationships of alternatives to characteristics to outcomes or benefits are analyzed.

For the access analysis, staff develops twenty-five community subgroups by identifying five types of individuals: recent high school graduates, currently employed adults, disadvantaged and racial and ethnic minorities, the retired and elderly, and women; each group resides in five socioeconomically homogenous geographical areas. Each of the five alternatives is assessed for its impact on the access of each of the twenty-five subgroups.

Extensive study, involving community advisory groups as well as college staff results in the rankings shown in Table 12.

Table 12.
RANKINGS OF POLICY ALTERNATIVES FOR
DISTRICT OPERATING MODE

Alternatives	Benefits	Costs (Ratio to least cost)	Access
A	4	1.00	5
B	2	1.30	4
C	5	1.15	3
D	1	1.25	2
E	3	1.08	1

Alternative C is automatically rejected because it ranks lowest on benefits and only average in costs and access. Alternative A is least expensive; private transportation time and out-of-pocket cost results in it being least effective in promoting student access. Alternative B is expensive because costs are measured in present discounted terms (with the present more highly valued than the future) and the need to start a second comprehensive campus with all the standard investments for utilities, site development, library, and gymnasium. The costs of alternative E are held down by inexpensive lease of otherwise unused community facilities and by limiting the number of courses taught in the neighborhood centers, thus insuring relatively large class sizes and using part-time faculty, paid at lower unit rates than full-time contract faculty. While quite accessible and providing transportation for second, third, and possibly later term undertakings at the central campus, the limited offerings give alternative E an average rank in benefits. Alternative D is attractive but expensive due to the fixed costs of three separate campuses and the opportunity costs of unused capacity at the first campus.

These results may lead policymakers to reject the traditional alternatives A, B, and C and consider D and E, which have not yet been high among college planning solutions. Since D is so expensive, the next step is to determine steps to improve E, so that benefits are increased without raising costs to an undesirable point.

Both the examples of deciding on programs for the elderly and for a long-range operating mode emphasize a problem frequently faced by decisionmakers: improvements in access or equity are often obtained only at the expense of decreasing economic efficiency, usually through increased costs but sometimes also by decreases in the quality of existing programs from which resources may need to be taken.

A major goal of current planning and development is that (*Theme One*) the basic nature of community college planning for the next several decades should switch from the facilities emphasis of the sixties to an emphasis on increasing access. Little or no growth in enrollment, pressures to develop new occupational curricula, less certain financial support for new programs, staff, and facilities, and changes in the very nature of the student body all make it necessary that (*Theme Two*) the notion of a comprehensive community college be modified and give way to that of a comprehensive community college *education*. The physical campus will be utilized as only one unit of a community system for delivering a comprehensive education; other units will involve extensive use of off-campus, non-college facilities and experience. The comprehensive community college education will also make extensive use of electronic media for delivering instruction on campus, at off-campus centers, and at remote locations. Community colleges will be more explicit in their planning of (*Theme Three*) education for multiple adult roles. The traditional community college functions of general education, transfer programs, occupational education, and adult and continuing education may be redefined in terms of adult functions. Courses and programs leading to self-improvement in adult roles, and of more direct benefit to the individual than to society, might include parent education, personal finance, education for recreation or leisure, and such personal skills as typing, dressmaking, and speech. Other courses and programs of self-development should improve the functioning of the individual in society, as a citizen-voter, taxpayer, consumer, conserver of resources, and volunteer worker in civic or service organizations. Supporting services would include counseling and other student services, remedial or developmental programs, and community service activities which do not fall within the scope of the other functions. This is in harmony with the concept (*Theme Four*) that comprehensive community college education requires more time, more options, and more outcomes.

Access must be made easy (*Theme Five*) for nontraditional students. Colleges which are able to remove barriers to access to campuses may still face the problem of not having courses and programs in which nontraditional students can succeed and are interested. Barriers to access can be lowered by developing alternatives to large central campuses, lecture-recitation methods of instruction, and rigidly prescribed curricula. Administrative barriers can also be reduced or removed altogether. Unrealistic deadlines and small fees constitute types of administrative barriers which are simple to remove.

Finally, to be effective, community college planning must be comprehensive; academic, fiscal, and physical planning must be coordinated, and federal, state, and local-institutional planning must be integrated appropriately (*Theme Six*). A caveat to this last theme is that primary responsibility for decisions about goals and priorities rests with local boards for community colleges in most states, within some general framework of state guidelines and goals. The extent to which access is expanded or improved, and the preferred modes for doing so, are ultimately within the scope of the decisions to be made at the local level.

These themes reflect the developments that are likely to take place in community colleges over the next quarter century. Planning and development will be markedly different than it now is, but it will still be needed. The models we suggest may require modifications in specific situations, but planners and analysts can use the approach both now, in an era of rapid change, and in the future, when present goals are reached and new themes are generated.

References

ADAMS AND MEIDAM. "Economics, Family Structure, and College Attendance." *American Journal of Sociology,* 74, No. 3, 1968 230–239.

ALLEN, A. "Taxonomy of Higher Education Barriers and Interventions for Minority and Low Income Students." *Journal of Black Studies,* March 1971, *1,* 357–366.

ALLPORT, G. W.; VERNON, P. E.; AND LINDZEY, G. *A Study of Values: Manual.* 3rd Ed. Boston: Houghton Mifflin, 1960.

ARNEY, L. H. *State Patterns of Financial Support for Community Colleges.* Gainesville: University of Florida, Institute of Higher Education, 1970.

ASTIN, A. W. "The Measured Effects of Higher Education." *Annals of the American Academy of Political and Social Science,* November 1972, 404, 1–20.

Carnegie Commission on Higher Education. *Less Time, More Options: Education Beyond the High School.* New York: McGraw-Hill, 1971a.

Carnegie Commission on Higher Education. *New Students and New Places: Policies for the Future Growth and Development of American Higher Education.* New York: McGraw-Hill, 1971b.

Carnegie Commission on Higher Education. *The Fourth Revolution:*

Instructional Technology in Higher Education. New York: McGraw-Hill, 1972.

Carnegie Commission on Higher Education. *College Graduates and Jobs: Adjusting to a New Labor Market Situation.* New York: McGraw-Hill, 1973.

Center for the Study of Higher Education. *Omnibus Personality Inventory: Research Manual.* Berkeley: University of California, 1962.

CIRCLE, D. "The Future Student at Brookdale." In R. Yarrington (Ed.), *Educational Opportunity for All: An Agenda for National Action.* Washington, D.C.: American Association of Community and Junior Colleges, 1973.

Coordinating Council for Higher Education. *Northeastern California Higher Education Study: A Report Prepared for the California Rural Consortium and the California Coordinating Council for Higher Education.* Council Report 72–7. Sacramento, 1972.

CROSS, K. P. *Beyond the Open Door: New Students to Higher Education.* San Francisco: Jossey-Bass, 1971.

CROSSLAND, F. E. *Minority Access to College: A Ford Foundation Report.* New York: Schocken, 1971.

DEEGAN, A. "Management by Management." *The Management of Personnel Quarterly,* Spring 1967, *6,* 16–20.

DEEGAN, W., GRIPP, T., JOHNSON, M., AND MC INTYRE, C. *Community College Management by Objectives.* Huntington Beach, Calif.: Stillwater Press, 1974.

Diridon Research Corporation. *A Survey of Attitudes Toward Higher and Continuing Education in Northeastern California.* San Jose, Calif., 1972.

DROR, E. *Public Policymaking Reexamined.* San Francisco: Chandler, 1968.

DRUCKER, P. *The Practice of Management.* New York: Harper and Row, 1954.

DRUCKER, P. "Integration of People and Planning." *Harvard Business Review,* November–December 1955, *33,* 35–40.

FERRIN, R. I. *A Decade of Change in Free-Access Higher Education.* New York: College Entrance Examination Board, 1971.

GLENNY, L. A., AND HURST, J. "Current Statewide Planning Structures and Powers." In L. A. Glenny and G. Weathersby (Eds.), *Statewide Planning for Postsecondary Education: Issues and Design.* Boulder, Colo.: National Center for Higher Education Management Systems, 1971.

GULKO, W. W. *Program Classification Structure.* Boulder: National Center for Higher Education Management Systems, Technical Report 27, 1972.

HEFFERLIN, JB L. "The Challenge to Planners of Trends in Postsecondary Education and Society." In L. A. Glenny and G. Weathersby (Eds.), *Statewide Planning for Postsecondary Education: Issues and Design.* Boulder, Colo: National Center for Higher Education Management Systems, 1971.

Higher Education Program Staff. *Higher Education Measurement and Evaluation KIT. Field Ed.* Los Angeles: Center for the Study of Evaluation, University of California, 1971.

HITT, W. D. *Increasing the Effectiveness of Educational Management in Community Colleges.* Mimeographed. Columbus, Ohio: Battelle Institute, 1972.

HUCKFELDT, V. *A Forecast of Changes in Postsecondary Education.* Boulder: National Center for Higher Education Management Systems, 1972.

HURLBURT, A. S. *State Master Plans for Community Colleges.* Washington: American Association for Community and Junior Colleges, Monograph No. 8, 1969.

KAHN, H. AND WIENER, A. J. *The Year 2000: A Framework for Speculation on the Next Thirty-Three Years.* New York: Macmillan, 1967.

KNOELL, D. M. *Toward Educational Opportunity for All.* Albany: State University of New York, 1966.

KNOELL, D. M. "Are Our Colleges Really Accessible to the Poor?" *Junior College Journal,* October 1968, *39,* 9–11.

KNOELL, D. M. *Black Student Potential: A Summary of the Study "People Who Need College: A Report on Students We Have Yet to Serve."* Washington, D.C.: American Association of Junior Colleges, 1970.

LAHTI, R. F. "Management by Objectives." *College and University Business,* July 1971, *52,* 31–33.

LAHTI, R. F. "Implementing the System Means Learning to Manage Your Objectives." *College and University Business,* February 1972, *52,* 43–46.

LOCKWOOD, G. "Planning a University." *Higher Education,* November 1972, *1,* 409–434.

MARTYN, K. *Increasing Opportunities for Disadvantaged Students: Final Report.* Unpublished. California Legislature, Joint Committee on Higher Education, Sacramento, 1969.

MEDSKER, L. L., AND TILLERY, D. *Breaking the Access Barriers: A Profile of Two-Year Colleges.* New York: McGraw-Hill, 1971.

MITCHELL, J. M., AND MITCHELL, W. C. *Political Analysis and Public Policy: An Introduction to Political Science.* Chicago: Rand McNally, 1969.

National Education Association Educational Policies Commission. *Universal Opportunity for Education Beyond the High School.* Washington, D.C.: 1964.

Northwest Regional Education Laboratory. *Innovative Instruction in Higher Education: A Project Report for the Oregon Coordinating Council.* Portland, 1973.

PALOLA, E., LEHMANN, T., AND BLISCHKE, W. R. *Higher Education by Design:* The Sociology of Planning. Berkeley: Center for Research and Development in Higher Education, 1970.

PETERSON, M. W. "Decision Type, Structure and Process Evaluation: A Contingency Model." *Higher Education,* May 1972, *1,* 207–221.

RAINES, M. R., AND MYRAN, G. A. *Community Services in the Community Colleges: Goals for 1980.* Mimeographed. East Lansing: Michigan State University, 1970.

SIMON, H. *Administrative Behavior.* New York: Free Press, 1965.

Technology and the American Economy: A Report of the National Commission on Technology, Automation, and Economic Progress. Vol. 1. Washington, D.C.: U.S. Government Printing Office, 1966.

TOFFLER, A. *Future Shock.* New York: Random House, 1970.

TOPPING, J. R. AND MIYATAKI, G. K. *Program Measures.* Boulder: National Center for Higher Education Management Systems, Technical Report 35, 1973.

TULLOCK, G. "Federalism: Problems of Scale." *Public Choice,* Spring 1969, *6.*

VON WEIZSACKER, C. C. "Problems in the Planning of Higher Education." *Higher Education,* November 1972, *1,* 391–408.

WILDAVSKY, A. "Rescuing Policy Analysis from PPBS." *Public Administration Review,* March–April 1969, *29,* 189–202.

WING, P. *Statewide Measures.* Overview and Guide. Boulder: National Center for Higher Education Management Systems (Preliminary Draft), 1973.

WING, P. AND TSAI, Y. *Report of a Survey of Current Enrollment Forecasting Practices of State Higher Education Agencies.* Boulder:

National Center for Higher Education Management Systems, 1973.

YARRINGTON, R. (Ed.) *Educational Opportunity for All: An Agenda for National Action.* Washington, D.C.: American Association of Community and Junior Colleges, 1973.

Index

145